CAREGIVER CAROLS: A MUSICAL, EMOTIONAL MEMOIR

by Don Wendorf, Psy.D.

DEDICATION To Susan:

"Grow old along with me, the best is yet to be"
Before we wed you quoted Browning's famous lines to me.
Over forty years have passed, not like I thought they'd be.
But, you remain my loving wife and fav'rite caregivee.

ACKNOWLEDGEMENTS

There are tons of people who have helped and continue to help Susan and me in all this caregiving, but I do want to say a special "thank you" to Sabra McCurdy, Genie and Jim Deason, Micky Graber, Linda Stutzman, Marian Stutzman, Alice Brumbach, Rosemary Gehman, Nancy Womble, Amber Scott and the kind ladies of the HomeInstead agency who all have spent hours doing hands on care. And, I can never thank my family enough for all the help and support you give us: sons Paul and David, daughters-in-law Christina and Jennifer and their families (Maria, Don, Don, Pat, Bob), sister Flo, brother Bob and sister-in-law Margaret. We get lots of long distance caring from Susan's sister, Carol, brother-in-law Bob, nephews Jeff and Gil and their wives Kathy and Dyann. Y'all will never know how much your love means to us. Thanks to my Shades Mountain Air bandmates, Gary Furr, Greg and Nancy Womble, and Melanie Rogers for being so understanding and accommodating with our needs that limit what the band can do.

As the Beatles sang long ago, "I {"we" actually} get by with a little help from my {"our"} friends." We get unbelievable amounts of love and encouragement from: Pat and Jackie, Steve and Lenora, Tonya and Jeremy, Rob and Kathy, Herb, Linda, Hank and Jan, Bert and Lindsay, Nita, Alan, Renee, Sherry, Janie, Dan, Vickie, Read, Tim, etc., etc. We appreciate so much our ever-faithful neighbors who check on us all the time: Heather, Rex and Lori, Blake and Erin, Pitsa and Jim, Carolyn, Josh and his family. Thanks to our medical people and their staffs who keep us going: Linda Hudson, David O'Neal, Jim Belyeu, Jo Lynne Herzog, Danalynn Guasteferro, Perron Tucker and Donna. Thanks to so many of my former clients who added their compassion, especially Debbie who helped us find out what Susan has in the first place.

I particularly want to thank some dear folks for assistance getting this book ready. Thank you supervision group, Jim Cotton, Robbin McInturff, Judi Schulman-Miller, and Bart Grooms, for your most insightful feedback. And thanks Sis (fellow author Flo Fitzpatrick) for the tech support on computer, formatting, editing and publishing issues as well as giving me new ideas and observations.

And, most of all, thanks to you Suze, for putting up with my writing and the time it takes in the midst of taking care of you and being willing for me to tell our story to be able to help others. That's just another fine example of the giving person you are.

TABLE OF CONTENTS

- 8   Introduction
- 14   Our Story as a Couple
- 27   Painted Bits of Bark and Stone and Tin
- 31   A Quarter of an Inch at a Time
- 34   Our Story as a Caregiver/Cargivee Couple
- 43   DNA-Did Not Assess
- 46   Heart-eyes
- 49   I Can Do It All
- 53   Too Much To Think
- 56   Caregiving Hero
- 58   Caregiving Burnout
- 61   Gimmicks in Limericks
- 66   One Bite at a Time
- 69   "Coffee and a Peace of I Please"
- 72   'Umble
- 74   Predictably Unpredictable

77	Up the Creek Without a GPS
80	Coach Talk
82	Proud Out Loud
85	Pride Inside
87	It's a Small World
89	Eyes on Demise
92	Who's Disabled Here?
95	Balk Talk
99	Hormonally Conflicted
102	How Do You Like Them Apples
104	And Another Thing
106	Living the Wife Life
109	Must Play Not to Win
113	On Sharing Bodily Fluids
115	Cherish or Perish
117	Guilty, Your Honor
120	It's Hard to Be the Caregivee
122	Sexed, Vexed and Perplexed
124	Smarter Martyr
126	Sweargiving

131 The Kindness of Friends We Don't Know

133 Unduly Muley?

137 Gravity is After Me

139 Vile Denial

142 Serial Grieving

145 Save 'Em For the End

150 Less Than Great Expectations

154 Do I Love Her, More or Less?

158 Feelings Fatigue

160 A Mile in Her Moccasins

163 Finale

168 Appendix: Susan Eulogy

INTRODUCTION

Hello and welcome to CAREGIVER CAROLS: A MUSICAL, EMOTIONAL MEMOIR. As in most memoirs, I'll tell you our story: the story of Susan and me as a couple and then as caregiver and disabled wife. But, my focus here is the **emotional** journey I've been on in taking care of Susan as she became increasingly dependent on others due to her strokes and resulting brain damage. I'll mostly be talking about my **feelings** in taking care of Susan, but I'll draw on insights gleaned from my 40 plus years as a psychologist/marriage and family therapist, where I worked with many other caregivers and chronically ill or disabled people, in addition to my own experience helping to take care of my mother-in-law, father and mother. I hope to accomplish several goals for the other caregivers reading this book:

1. To let you experience through understanding my feelings, that although they may often be very complex and intense, and sometimes unpleasant, difficult or not very pretty, **your emotions are normal**. I hope that hearing some of my emotions will help you be more aware of your own, recognize and name them and comprehend them more fully.

2. To let you see that other caregivers are struggling with the same sort of emotions, **You are not alone.** There are others who can understand, accept and give you support and help and I strongly, strongly, strongly encourage you to seek them out and **ask for their assistance** or receive it gracefully when it's offered.

3. To help you find ideas for how **you can manage your feelings** better, mostly from understanding more about where they come from, examining your concepts and assumptions about them and seeing

how you might try thinking about them in fresh, new, more productive ways, so you can modify your actions or decisions.

4. It may sound kind of odd, but I hope **you will feel some comfort or reassurance or encouragement or companionship** just from reading about my emotions. Maybe you'll recognize something you've felt, too, or think "Wow, I guess it's o.k. I feel this 'cause he does, too." Maybe you'll discover you've been assuming something was one emotion when it was really something else or came from some other issue or dynamic. Hopefully, some things will trigger new thoughts in you such as: "That gives me an idea of how I might deal with this issue differently." Perhaps you'll forget your own struggles for a moment and be glad you don't experience something I do or you may feel compassion for me and then for yourself or even think, "Hey, I'm handling that lots better than he is." You may get a more accurate level on your own emotions by comparing them with mine.

    I will not be providing you with lists of simple, practical, quick, easy things to do to make everything nice and peachy keen, because I don't think there are any and I don't think it's reasonable to expect all the emotional struggles to be resolved or go away. I wish they would; but, I think the nature of this caregiving enterprise is that for most of us there will always be some tough times and tough personal issues to grapple with. The goal is to manage them the best you can, not eliminate them all. As a psychologist, I used to make a distinction between difficulties and problems. Difficulties are troublesome things but they don't have solutions that just make them vanish. Problems also have to be addressed but they need to be solved. It's important to recognize which you're dealing with, as attempts to "solve" difficulties rather than just cope with them, usually result in making them worse or turning them into sure enough problems that are a natural part of life or life circumstances. They have to be dealt with.

For example, it really is a problem that Susan can not feed, bathe or toilet herself. Those tasks have to be accomplished just to stay alive. My reactions in doing these for her, like frustration, impatience, anxiety, or irritation, are difficulties I have to learn to manage the best I can so they don't drive either of us nuts. But, if I think I can and must find a way to stop *feeling* them, I'm in trouble, because they probably **will** recur. That, I'm afraid, is the nature of things and they go with this territory. Expecting and trying to get rid of them altogether may lead to increased anger, discouragement and even depression. I'm afraid we have to accept that we **will** repeatedly experience some emotions that are very hard; that we will sometimes do better with them and sometimes worse; but that they are the same sort of stuff everybody else has to face because we are all just human.

Most of our significant relationships have some chronic, unresolved difficulties. Most marriages — and Susan's and mine is no exception — have some issues we go round and round on for years or forever. We are different people, with different backgrounds and childhoods and needs and feelings and experiences and ideas, and it is not easy to combine those into a relationship, especially one so powerful as marriage. You will undoubtedly spot a few of those as we proceed, such as my difficulty of feeling I often can't please Susan or please her enough. Similarly, most parent-child relationships have a legacy of some hurts or unfilled needs or unsettled conflicts or unforgiven injuries. One of the hardest things to do is to lovingly take care of someone who we feel fell short in taking care of us in the past. These difficulties are unlikely to be automatically resolved just through the enterprise of caregiving a spouse or parent; but, they are extremely likely to to be tapped into. I'd expect some if I were you. And, they may offer an opportunity to make some headway in coming to peace with them and even healing or strengthening a relationship. But, you may also have to accept that you are not going to get some of the caring, loving, justice, validation, need fulfillment, acceptance, etc., that you have always sought or deserved. So, try to keep them at the level of "difficulties" and not turn them into "problems."

I also want this book to be useful to people who are being taken care of, as well as to the family and friends of caregivers. Hopefully, it will provide them with some understanding of what you, the caregiver, is going through so they may know better how to relate to you, especially during the emotionally rough periods. Maybe it will provoke some additional outpourings of support, empathy and assistance, too. Many of you will be able to engage your caregivee in discussions about what this experience is like for them, which could open up all kinds of possibilities and changes and growth.

And, finally, **I wrote this to help take care of myself**, too: to have a place to get my feelings out; a creative enterprise to give my mind a safe refuge to retreat to; and a chance to examine my emotions and behavior and understand them better through this endeavor to express myself clearly and artistically. It has done all that for me and, since you're reading this, it means I must have resolved my issues with having other people know such personal things about Susan and me. It's funny, but I have felt more comfortable with the idea of strangers reading this than my own friends, and particularly my own family. I have felt very ashamed of my angry outbursts and frequent lack of kindness and I sure didn't want my kids to know I had [gasp] **sexual** feelings, although I think they may have suspected it once they grew up. I say all this because I want to strongly encourage you to seek outlets and ways of expression for yourself. I hope you will consider writing a journal of your own feelings and experiences or your own poems, songs, plays, essays, blogs, etc.

This book, like my previous one, *Love Lyrics: The Musical Marital Manual*, is primarily written in a song lyric/rhyming light verse format, with some brief prose commentary accompanying each selection. I have been a psychologist/marriage and family therapist and a performing musician all my adult life. I chose this medium because I think we all accept, absorb, remember and utilize information more easily if it comes in an engaging, entertaining, emotional, metaphorical and aesthetic experience. Despite our best efforts to be a rational species, we homo sapiens are far more emotional critters than we are usually aware of or want to be or are comfortable in being. So, I use this more emotional/artistic/experiential format to inform and give a feeling for what I want to convey. I hope you find this format enjoyable as well as helpful, because the topic itself isn't especially fun.

I'm not figuring on this being unusually inspirational, overly optimistic, or pessimistic, or particularly wise or insightful. Some of these feelings are tough, grim, scary, raw, confusing, embarrassing, intimate, frustrating, discouraging. So, I've tried to put as much lightness, irony, and humor, plus puns and funny rhymes into it as I could without being disrespectful. As Mary Poppins said, "A spoonful of sugar helps the medicine go down" and humor helps us put things in perspective. Humor involves us looking down on something from a new, outside angle and saying, "Whew, boy, ain't that weird?" But, I intend for this to be real, very real, or it won't be helpful. So, I'm not going to gloss or minimize or put too much make up on it. I'm not trying to present myself as the ideal example of how to be a caregiver and I will often come across looking pretty bad. Unfortunately, I think you'll gain the most from my mistakes and struggles. Lots of my issues are unresolved and probably will remain so, some maybe forever. Remember, too, that these are MY feelings and some of yours may be quite different; I hope **lots** of them are. Don't think that you are "supposed" to feel the same things I have or that there is something wrong if your feelings are not like mine. The focus needs to be on your relating my feelings to YOUR feelings so you get the benefits. That's why I wrote the book: I want you to be able to cope with your caregiving the best you can. I will try to help you find new ways to understand, think about, experience, label, evaluate, act upon and shift your emotions.

Now, let me tell you a STORY:

Susan and me dating in 1968

OUR STORY AS A COUPLE

    Susan Elizabeth Black grew up in Dallas, Texas where she was born on 12/03/1946. Her father, Bob Black, was an accountant for the Texas & Pacific railroad. He was a tall, slender, quiet, reserved man of Scottish extraction who smoked a pipe and reportedly, never got very angry. His father, "Dad," was born in Scotland; spoke with a heavy brogue; and came over often to garden at Susan's house and teach her how to garden. Gardening was to become one of her great passions as an adult. I never met Bob Black, as he had died of a heart attack related to a congenital heart defect the week of her high school graduation in 1965; but, all the family legends describe him as one of the nicest and most gentle of men you'd ever hope to meet. Regarding Bob and Dad, Susan's sister Carol, told me, "I never heard either of them speak an unkind word." Bob and his ghost are a tough act to follow and I've always referred to him as "Saint Robert." I think the story is that he was very attracted to Susan's mother, a tall, pretty, outgoing divorcee with two little girls, and he went to the doctor she worked for as a secretary. But, he was rather timid and shy in his pursuit, so much so that she had to push things along a little bit. Susan's mother, Virginia, better known as "Jenny," went to secretarial school and then got a nursing degree after Bob died and did her best to raise her kids by herself, despite having breast cancer shortly thereafter. It took two more cancers and a quadruple bypass to finally stop "Mama" many years later, I'm pleased to say, as I was very close to Mama. Susan had one half- sister, Lee, seven years older who was also very pretty and had a lovely singing voice, but lots of problems. Susan also had a second mother in her oldest half-sister, Carol who would later be known to our kids as "Crazy Old Aunt Carol" as she shared their mother's zany, unpredictable sense of humor. Carol married, had two sons (Jeff and Gil), got divorced and took care of herself and the boys, continuing to work after she married to Bob Hamilton, whom I would later refer to as "Mr. Hospitality" for his kindness to all of us. His poetry also inspired the format for my first book, a self-help marriage manual.

Susan grew up surrounded by aunts and lots of cousins to play with. In hard times, lots of those relatives shared their homes with each other. The top half of Susan's house burned down one time, but Mama's resilience and sense of humor got them all through it and she ended up playing piano for everyone who came to help. Mama also played accordion and organ, but she was best on the harmonica (I still play three of her mouth harps). After high school, Susan went to Baylor University in Waco, Texas, later shifting up to the Baylor nursing program in Dallas. She dropped out of nursing school after fainting at the gook and gore of her first several patients. She'd planned to become a nurse and go to Viet Nam: maybe a tad bit idealistic. While in school in Dallas she'd been assaulted by a would-be rapist who got as far as banging her head on the pavement, causing some left temporal brain damage visible decades later on her first MRI, before someone drove up and he ran off. Her sister Lee was plagued with a psychiatric illness, probably bipolar disorder, and Susan had spent much of her life being Lee's "angel" and emotional caregiver. This intensified as Susan continued college in American Studies at Baylor in Waco and she often made emergency trips to Dallas to help Lee. At times she'd escape all the crazy phone calls to spend a few days at the home of an extraordinarily kind English professor, who also played trombone (my father's instrument) in the Baylor jazz band where I was the drummer.

I was born two days before Christmas in 1947 during what, until very recently, was the worst blizzard in New York history. My brother, Bob, and I were the first twins to receive a complete blood transfusion at birth, necessary for Rh blood problems with our parents. Mom and Pop lost their first two children to those problems; so, you can imagine how thrilled they were to have Bob and me. Our father, Hulen, was then in the Army and our first home was New Haven where the Army was sending him through Yale Law School after he returned from the South Pacific in World War II. Pop grew up in West, Texas (yes, where the fertilizer plant blew up in 2013), a little Czech community 15 miles north of Waco, although my grandparents were of German stock. My great, great-grandfather was from Kiel, Germany, but there is another little town actually named "Wendorf." Grandpa ran a lumber yard, was postmaster and a volunteer fireman (our son David is now a firefighter), and later had his own wallpaper and paint store. He was a strict teetotaller and the West dominos champ. Pop had one brother, Eddie, who became a Navy pilot and was a World War II ACE and war hero. After Yale, Pop became Army JAG and I spent my first 12 years as an Army brat, living in Mt. Vernon, Va.; Orleans, France; Ft. Stewart, Ga., and Alexandria, Va. until he retired.

After a couple of years in private practice in El Paso, Texas, he moved us all to Waco so he could teach law at Baylor and take care of his aging parents in nearby West.

"Us all" included our younger sister Florence, named after Mom's mother and younger sister. "Sis," as Bob and I call her, has always had a passion for dance and musical theater, maybe as Mom and Pop courted dancing to all the Big Band era bands at West Point where they met and then danced all their lives together. Sis earned a degree in dance and another in musical theatre, but has been most successful as an author of romance/ mystery/suspense books under the name of Flo Fitzpatrick (check her out: she's **very** good). Mom and her five siblings lived at where their Army father was the chief medical officer. Mom's ancestors are also German except for one Irish Ryan (Grandma) who snuck in there somehow.

Pop got to West Point from a military prep school or "honor school" in Bryan, Texas where he'd been accepted as he played trombone (valve, not slide until our Dixieland band years later)and doubled on violin which he learned from his music teacher Aunt Jo. They had a big band, "Doc Mize and his Cadets: the South's Finest College Dance Band," and this was the Big Band era as you'll recall. My folks married in 1939 after his West Point graduation. Mom, although very intelligent, did not want to go to college (perhaps due to her shyness/social anxiety) and spent her life as a wife, mother and homemaker, with a passion for home decorating and Catholicism (when the Pope had doubts, he called Mom). I should mention that Mom's name was "Mary" (Grandma wanted to name her "Mari" but spelled it "M- a-r-i-e" and Mom changed it later to "Mary." My only granddaughter is now named "Mari" or "Mari Carmen," actually). Mom also loved *taking care of* "little old ladies" and she always had one or two she would take shopping or to church or would clean their houses while she had Bob and me mow their lawns. Unfortunately, I never really learned to dance very well, maybe because Pop got a band started at our small parochial high school and Bob and I joined the band: Bob on sousaphone and me on drums. We soon started our own rock band (Bob taught himself bass violin) and so I played for other people to dance. After high school, Bob and I both went to Baylor and decided to major in psychology.

O.K. now we're ready for Susan and me to meet. As seniors, in the Fall of 1968, Bob and I had moved into an apartment on the edge of the Baylor campus, although our family still lived in Waco. That first day in our apartment we bumped into our friend Amber who lived across the street in a big old house. We had had a number of honors courses together and she was excited to be our neighbor. She invited us over to meet her three roommates. I remember climbing up her stairs and at the top of the steps was Susan. Wow! Something happened. I didn't even care about meeting the other two, although Amber and two of the other roomies, Renee and Sherry, have remained our friends to this day (no surprise: she's still friends with Glenda, the first girl she met in first grade). As it turned out, Susan and I also had an economics class together that semester and had to walk the same direction after that to our next classes. So, I saw her at least every Monday, Wednesday and Friday and always walked with her across campus after class. I also found reasons to visit across the street. Lots of reasons; not to mention Amber's good cooking.

I was extremely attracted to Susan right from the get-go. She was physically beautiful to me, with a pretty face, long blonde hair, and a slender figure. She's never thought she was pretty, but I've always **known** she was (Sis describes her as a cross between Greta Garbo and Vanessa Redgrave). But, I was even more taken by her personality, her character and her spirit. She had an air of sweetness and caring about her and I soon came to realize she was one of the most accepting, giving, forgiving and loving people I had ever known. She didn't talk in super-religious jargon, despite a conservative Southern Baptist background, but she exuded a living spirituality that seemed very real and desirable. She had deeply-felt religious beliefs; I had deeply-felt religious doubts, having recently emerged from my Catholic upbringing. But we seemed to have an essential connection in our understanding of the importance of people and the sanctity of life. I also found Susan to be very bright and fun and very comfortable to be with. We shared lots of interests and values in common, especially in our concern about people in need or pain. We both anticipated a simple lifestyle full of family, friends and service to others. We talked about some day founding "people schools" to teach children how to be loving humans and maybe even adopting or fostering kids.

    I probably would have proposed to her after the first five minutes, but, I had understood that she was dating Brian and I was too timid (I inherited Mom's shyness/ social anxiety although I am *extroverted* shy) and chivalrous to compete for her attentions (like Saint Robert?). It was clear we liked each other a lot and I tried to content myself with our walks and talks and neighbor get-togethers to become better friends until such time as she might become available. I was smitten...bad. But, we were both quite busy, with heavy class loads; she worked part-time to put herself through school; I was in the student congress and very active in campus protests against the Viet Nam war; and I played drums in four bands, including a jazz combo with Bob on bass, and a lousy, but fun Dixieland jazz band with my father (years later I was to play mandolin in a bluegrass band with my violinist son, Paul, and sometimes for events with the addition of my other son, David, on guitar or piano and me on hammered dulcimer; Bob's son Marc was later to play both bass and trombone while his other son Karl played saxophone like Sis did before her majorette days: little threads weaving around us).

We weren't any less busy the start of the Spring semester and I was more and more drawn to Susan. Then, through some kind of miracle: Brian became history!! She has claimed since that they were never really dating seriously anyway, which I wished I'd known at the time. At any rate, I immediately asked her out to a party. I think it was mostly a beer bash, but we were totally absorbed in talking with each other and missed most of the party. When I took her home, we shared a first kiss. I was a goner. I might have proposed then, too, but Spring break came early and I drove with Bob and three other buddies all the way to Boston and back...non-stop. Ahhhh, youth. I'll never forget my reunion with Susan when the break was over. I was reading under a tree and she spotted me and walked over. That special image and experience are what I describe in "Heart-eyes" in this book. She embraced me and I knew we were both falling in love, not just me. We saw each other as much as we could the rest of that semester and Summer before I had to leave in August 1969 to go to graduate school at Vanderbilt University in Nashville. I had gotten to know her mother and sisters and family in Dallas and she had gotten to know my parents and brother and Sis in Waco.

She recalls her first meeting with Mom when I brought her to my parents' house and Mom was up on a footstool painting the walls, dressed in her pearls and stockings (and girdle) and earrings and full makeup: the ultimate lady.

It was tough being away from Susan that first, very stressful semester at Vanderbilt. We called and wrote (people wrote *paper* letters in those days) and got together in Dallas or Waco when we could for holidays. She even visited once in Nashville, although she wouldn't use my disgusting bathroom until she had painted it (not hard as you could literally sit on the toilet, soak your feet in the tub and wash your hands in the sink simultaneously). I talked to her constantly in my head, so much so that I would forget to actually tell her things in reality, and I even had a small bottle of her Madame Rochas perfume I would smell to feel connected. Susan had a couple of courses to finish at Baylor and then moved back to Dallas with her mother, where she felt very captured and emotionally drained, especially as Lee's problems worsened. We limped through that year and I then began working full-time at a state psychiatric hospital in Nashville to do my two years of alternative civilian service as a conscientious objector. Susan was accepted in the University of Tennessee's branch campus in Nashville to pursue her masters degree in social work and so she moved and got a little apartment not too far from mine. I then did propose but she thought I was not ready: "too immature." I worked; she did graduate school and part-time work in several jobs, including house mother in a home for unwed expectant mothers (who climbed out the windows to see their boyfriends) and, our favorite: helping to open new Exxon stations by dressing in a tiger suit and giving out frozen chickens with a fill-up to promote their "put a tiger in your tank" campaign!

After another year, she decided I was ready to marry and I decided she was right: I was NOT ready to marry. We had grappled with our differences, particularly around religious backgrounds, over and over, even breaking up briefly several times in despair we could ever resolve them. These splits usually happened after all night deep, painful, intimate discussions that actually served to bring us closer at the same time. I finally realized I had to make up my mind to either make a commitment to make a marriage work no matter what it took or give up Susan altogether and forever. I couldn't tolerate the latter; so, in my VW bug, on I-35 just north of Abbott, Texas (home of

Willie Nelson whom she has now become obsessed with 40 years later) I proposed and she accepted. Whew. We married in a little chapel at Scarrit College in Nashville on 2/19/72 with just family and a few friends present. We moved together into a little log cabin in the Nashville suburbs: very cute and rustic. No AC: hot as hell. Susan finished her MSSW while I finished my hospital service. I had become totally disillusioned with Vanderbilt's Ph.D. program (great school but not a *clinically* oriented training program) and gotten accepted back in Baylor's new Psy.D. (Doctor of Psychology) professional psychology program on the condition that I had to start all over from the beginning. So, back to Waco. I did graduate school and Susan worked, including as an adoption worker for the Texas welfare system. My final year was a clinical internship and I was accepted at the University of Alabama at Birmingham. I then got a job in UAB's Department of Psychiatry, where I worked for the next five years. My brother Bob moved to Birmingham to work in a mental health center, where he met and eventually married Margaret. He started a private practice with a couple of other therapists and I left UAB to join them in 1984. We had had Paul at the end of the internship year and David came along three years later. Bob and Margaret had Karl and then Marc and we all made Birmingham our home.

    I developed my expertise in marriage and family therapy with additional training in supervision groups, putting on workshops, writing articles for professional journals, reading and attending seminars. I got involved in the Alabama Division of the American Association for Marriage and Family Therapy and held several elected offices. At the same time I was very involved with my music (I had left jazz drums for bluegrass guitar, mandolin and hammered dulcimer), first through the Magic City Slickers (Birmingham is the "Magic City") and then with Shades Mountain Air (my band of the last 16 years now). I also played a lot with our oldest son, Paul, who played violin and viola and enough guitar to be useful and sometimes with David, too, who played guitar and keyboards. Susan was very involved with raising kids, gardening, handling our finances and doing most of the house work. She was always active in church and loved doing things for other people: keeping their kids, fixing them meals, taking shut-in's to the store, etc.

She still found some time to do the handwork she'd always loved, such as crochet and cross-stitch and making people cards or encouraging notes like the "Painted Bits of Bark and Stone and Tin" I describe in the selection here by that name. We did a lot of camping with the boys and Susan got us into the Audubon society and bird-watching. Both boys played soccer and Paul played a little baseball and basketball; so, we spent a fair amount of time with that, as well as with their music and art lessons. Much of our childrearing was done in a 1977 Toyota station wagon we got the month Paul was born and later called "Old Blue" as it was still going (sort of) when Paul was 21.

When our boys were in middle school we moved Susan's mother from Dallas to an apartment a couple of blocks from our house because she had cancer again. Carol and her family had moved to San Antonio and Mama's siblings in Dallas had died. Susan did a lot of caregiving of her mother, with some help from me, along with eventually homeschooling the boys, which she did through high school. Mama recovered from that cancer and later had a quadruple bypass before finally dying of her third cancer when David was in high school. I felt good about our caregiving experience with Mama except that, after 25 years of our playing Scrabble together, she beat me with the highest single word score and game score either of us had ever had and then passed on without giving me a rematch! Tacky. Susan inherited her grandfather's love of gardening and had a beautiful raised bed, intensive French garden she is still proud of (my father was a big vegetable gardener and my brother is an expert Japanese gardener). I did the double digging (turn over two spade depths down) and she now won't let me cut down the trees that have grown up there on their own, to attest to the wonderfulness of her hard-worked soil. Both boys went to college locally at Samford University, where they each met their marvelous wives: Christina for Paul and Jennifer for David. David and Jenn soon gave us our first grandson, Fritz. David worked doing high-end remodeling carpentry and eventually became a firefighter, plus doing cabinet making on the side. Paul had left classical music in college, gotten an M.Div. at Beeson Seminary in town, and ended up as a policeman. Paul and Christina had Jack and Mari Carmen while still in Alabama and then Berin and Rowan after they moved to Texas with the FBI.

Before Paul et al. left, we had already moved my parents here from Waco in 2004 as Pop had Parkinson's disease and Mom was in early stages of Alzheimer's. My brother's older son, Karl, had been suffering horribly from bone cancer a couple of years already and required more and more caregiving, which exacted a terrible emotional toll from Bob and Margaret. He died a tragic, heroic death in 2004. Then Pop died in 2006, just a month short of his 90th birthday (we gave him a month's credit for in utero time so he could break the family longevity record). We had all helped in the caregiving with Mom and Pop, although I tried to do a little more since Karl needed Bob and Margaret so much. Mom's Alzheimer's gradually worsened and she required more and more care even though she eventually lived in an Alzheimer's unit. She remembered most of us until a few months before she died in April of 2012, while Susan and I were in Texas for grandson Berin's birth. We had closed down our private practice when Bob retired in 2007 and I went to work for my old friend Bert Pitts. I continued playing mandolin, mandola, guitar, clawhammer banjo, hammered dulcimer, harmonica and jews' harp (the first instrument Pop taught me to play in junior high) in my band, Shades Mountain Air, that Paul played violin in until he moved.

This brings us to the next and current chapter in our saga and the inspiration for this book. In 1995 I had begun noticing some changes in Susan. She began forgetting little things: a phone number or birthday or something she'd told me or I'd told her or an event from a couple of months ago and then, my being gone almost a week the year before to go to Texas to buy a Toyota from Carol and Bob. She could drive to point A or to point B but started having trouble figuring how to drive from A to B. Once, she had to plot an alternate route back from her dentist due to a detour and she drove to Sylacauga, some 30 miles away before she realized she was lost. Finally, we started pursuing some medical evaluation, seeing a neurologist and a neuropsychologist, which got the diagnosis that changed all our lives forever.

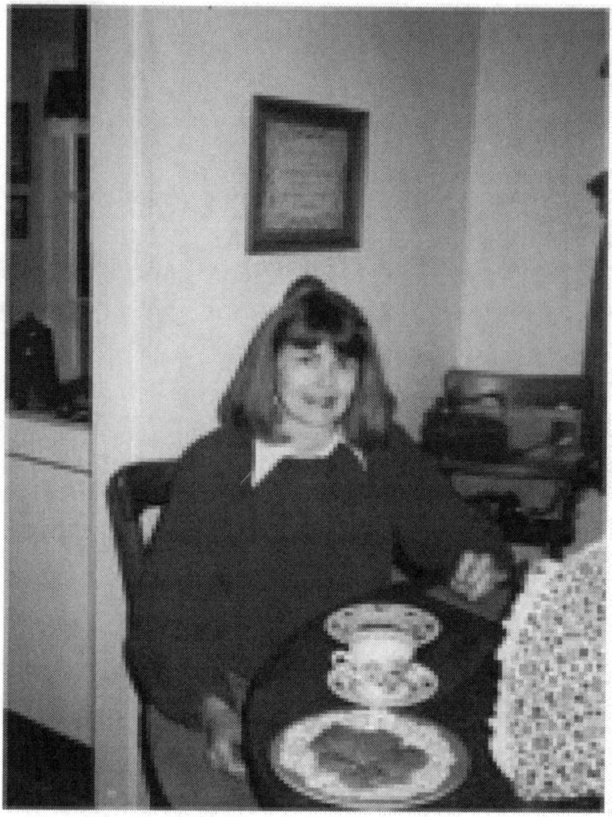

PAINTED BITS OF BARK AND STONE AND TIN

She won my heart in college when she lived across the street.
Her roommate was a friend of mine, who thought that we should meet.
I liked her looks and kindness, but what made our love begin,
Was her painted bits of bark and stone and tin.

I'd leave for class each morning and come back again at dark,
To find she'd left a love note, painted on a piece of bark,
Or maybe on a shiny rock, I'd spot as I walked in:
Her painted bits of bark and stone and tin.

She'd stop and chat on campus when I'd study 'neath a tree,
And when she'd leave I'd open up my book again to see,
A sweet verse on a rusted tin can lid she'd slipped within:
More painted bits of bark and stone and tin.

"Grow old along with me," she wrote, "the best is yet to be."
That Browning poem that she'd quote proved true for her and me.
Who'd guess that such a little rhyme would lifetime love begin,
From painted bits of bark and stone and tin.

We married, raised two sons, and shared together forty years.
But now her health is slipping fast, the end of her life nears.
So it's my turn to care for her and keep love flowing in,
Bring her painted bits of bark and stone and tin.

I know that I must let her go, release her from my heart;
Let Present stop our Past, so our Forever love can start.
But I'd give all I treasure for that pleasure once again,
Of her painted bits of bark and stone and tin.
I'll let our Now end up our Then, our Always to begin,
Clutching painted bits of bark and stone and tin.

I wrote this song during the time we still thought Susan had Alzheimer's and we were facing her gradual descent into oblivion and death. I recorded this and the next song, "A Quarter of an Inch at a Time," for a

Valentine's present, with the help of Nancy Womble and Gary Furr from my band, *Shades Mountain Air.* I saw the painted bits of bark and stone and tin as a pretty good metaphor for who Susan's always been: an extremely caring, giving person who loved to reach out to support and nurture and encourage others in simple little ways. One of the very hardest things for her to bear in losing most of her ability to use her arms, fingers and eyes has been this, and all the others things she loved to **do** for people. I've tried to convince her that she still can, and does, give the essence of what she always gave: her acceptance, compassion, empathy and affection, But she has to do it differently now, with the little physical ability she has left. She can still listen and talk, even if someone else has to dial and hold the phone. Her motto has always been, "bloom where you're planted." She's tried to keep this up, but it's become harder and harder, such that she'd now prefer to just be literally planted, as in six feet under. Actually, she's donating her body to a medical school. Her body donor card is one of her favorite possessions and she usually asks me if I have it when we go out somewhere. So, she's going to go out the way she's always been by giving what she has to give. This song now stirs up fondness along with a heavy dose of sadness and sympathy.

      The course of Susan's "Alzheimer's" did not follow the usual one and her diagnosis got changed to "fronto-temporal dementia," although the neurologist felt it didn't really fit that very well either. I was still working full-time at my practice and we limped along, with the help of our kids and then additional caregiving from a number of saintly women in our church, Grace and Truth. After a couple of years, one of my clients, Debbie C., told me about antiphospholipid antibody syndrome, which was easily diagnosed with a simple blood test. Susan tested positive and we learned that her brain damage was actually the result of a clotting problem that causes "mini-strokes" and some not so mini- strokes in her brain, resulting in seizures, hypertension, memory loss, impairment in motor and cognition and emotional functioning. This disorder is treated with blood thinners and she started on Coumadin, plus Depakote and Lamictal for the complex partial seizures, in addition to the Razadyne and Namenda she had already been taking for dementia. This all slowed down the progression of the disorder and dysfunction, although it could not reverse existing damage, and she has still had even more strokes that further impaired her coordination, visual processing and sense of location in space. She was still pretty much herself in personality and very aware of what she could no longer do. Her life became more and more boring and hard and mine became more busy and complicated while we both tried to bloom as well as we could.

The last couple of decades of life seem to have a lot to do with letting go, saying goodbye to people we care about and abilities we've always had. Grief specialists tell us that the final stage of bereavement is making the transition from a tangible, physical relationship to a spiritual bond with our deceased loved one. Many couples I saw in therapy told me they felt a spiritual bond with their living spouse, some even from the very first second they met. I'm not sure I understand how this happens or what this even means, but it feels right. Maybe that's how many "lifers" like us get to be "lifers" in the first place. And, if it's a spiritual bond, why couldn't it survive death? Maybe she'll be painting me bits of bark and stone and tin in Heaven. Meanwhile, I miss them.

I'm learning how to give Susan those painted bits, but hers need to be in different form. Somehow or the other, over the many years we've had together, she managed to become the ultimate Willie Nelson fan. So, I have bought her a slew of Willie CD's, concert videos, and books that we go through over and over (and over and over). For her 66th birthday I got us tickets to actually see her idol in person at the Alabama Theatre here in Birmingham. Our son, David, chauffered us, and I arranged handicapped seating on about the 6th row. Unfortunately, after Willie's kids, excellent musicians in their own rights, performed and she'd sat there freezing and way beyond her bedtime, she was only able to make it into song #5. But, she saw The Man. Painted bits of bark and stone and tin.

A QUARTER OF AN INCH AT A TIME

She moved near me in college, to the house across from mine.
I knew at once this special girl was something rare and fine.
We slowly started strolling down a path of love sublime:
A quarter of an inch at a time
A quarter of an inch at a time

Through kids, careers, through fights and fears, we formed a wedded pair,
That knew each other deeply as we learned to give and share,
Ever stronger, growing closer, like two trees entwine:
A quarter of an inch at a time
A quarter of an inch at a time

Then came a bandit in the night, to rob me of my bride,
To slowly steal away her brain and personhood inside,
To make her serve a lengthy sentence, punishing no crime:
A quarter of an inch at a time
A quarter of an inch at a time

I watch a shade be slowly drawn to darken out her will.
I see her memory erode, from mountain down to hill.
I hear my singer drift off key, my poet stray off rhyme:
A quarter of an inch at a time
A quarter of an inch at a time

This dearest soul I've ever met, so caring, sweet and kind,
So lovely on the outside with as lovely heart and mind,
Now works to hold the fabric of her self as it unwinds:
A quarter of an inch at a time
A quarter of an inch at a time

As man and wife we've walked through life, down all its winding roads,
Up craggy peak, 'cross desert bleak, we've borne each other's loads.
There's just this final mountain now, together we will climb:
A quarter of an inch at a time
A quarter of an inch at a time

This song, like the previous one, "Painted Bits of Bark and Stone and Tin," was recorded for Susan as a Valentine's present a number of years ago when we still thought she had Alzheimer's that would progress to total nothingness. I was still praying that she would just continue to know me and trust me so I could take care of her. Alzheimer's is a horrible, horrible disease. On the TV commercials it looks like all you have to do is pop a few medications and everyone is happy and doing just fine. The reality is that, as of the time I'm writing this, medications only maintain current functioning, but they do not stop the progressive death of brain cells. Eventually, everyone falls off the plateau. In the end, you die with this, but not before you slowly die as a person, along with all the relationships you've been a part of. You forget who you are, who everyone else is and how to do everything you've ever done. But, it happens painfully slowly, with a lot of confusion and anxiety along the way, as you struggle to hold on and make sense of what is happening: "a quarter of an inch at a time." The only redeeming part of it is that you may finally lose awareness of how awful things are. However, the people who love you and care for you still know you and search desperately for any little trace of you that can still be touched. No one should have to go through this but this disease now touches almost all of us in some way or other. I thought for several years that Susan and I were dealing with this and we did have to deal with this with my mother for ten years until she died with Alzheimer's in April of 2012. The last few months Mom had no idea who I was, who she was and what was going on. She was bewildered, frightened and alone.

It seems kind of strange reading this now,

when I'm more looking at an ever narrowing but never ending road stretching into nowhere. Susan and I are probably facing some more loss of function, if the last few years of a stroke or two a year, continue. But, Susan manages to hold onto most of Susan in her thinking, memory, personality, values and emotions. So, I'm scared about the changes we'll have to deal with as well as losing more of my own courage and patience. In the meantime, my heart goes out to all the victims of this disease and to you who are taking care of a loved one with all the patience, love and courage you can muster. You have my deepest respect and sympathy. You caregivers give a whole new dimension to the words "love" and "commitment." I hope you will honor and cherish yourself for what you do.

OUR STORY AS A CAREGIVER/CAREGIVEE COUPLE

I haven't been looking forward to writing this section. I reviewed lots of depressing and dreary and detailed medical records and notes (I saved too much and organized too little). It brought up lots of memories and reminded me of much I didn't remember and some things I didn't particularly care to remember. It all seemed like too much of too much and made me tired reading it: we've already been a **long** way on this trek. As I related earlier in telling about our individual and couple histories, I first started getting concerned about Susan as early as 1995, when she was just turning 50. She's had more than her share of medical issues all her life, including hypoglycemia or low blood sugar problems back to at least her adolescence and poor vision back to childhood. As a little girl she was highly allergic to cats, and took shots to be able to keep her cat, Amber (yes, same name as the college friend who introduced us, although this historical fact did not thrill the human Amber); but, that became less of an issue after Mama backed the car over the kitty. During our years of marriage, the hypoglycemia got worse; she tested positive for every allergen they could poke her with; she later got arthritic degeneration in her back and then her neck; her vision got poorer as she developed keratoconus (curvature of the cornea) and she had all sorts of problems with her blood pressure spiking all over the place. She also had some foot problems, possibly related to my running over the edge of one backing up the car (like Mama). And, don't forget the eczema, psoriasis and seborrheic dermatitis. So, we were used to dealing with her not being the healthiest of folks. Maybe we were too used to it as we probably misinterpreted some symptoms as stuff we knew, like hypoglycemic or blood pressure crises, when they later turned out to be new stuff we really needed to know correctly: her little strokes.

During 1995 she had some "vague syncopal" episodes when she had double vision, weakness and a spinning sensation while her blood pressure and blood sugar seemed fine. She'd appear to get better almost immediately when she took a glucose tablet as we'd done for years; but, this didn't look quite the same somehow. And, I started noticing her being forgetful. At first it was little things like grocery items or recipes or phone numbers(I always considered her to be a walking phone book). She'd repeat little things she'd already told me or forgot that we'd gone to a concert recently or that Paul had dislocated his shoulder the previous year falling off a trail bike (scary for a violinist). Over the next couple of years this got gradually worse. She forgot stories from her childhood that I knew from her telling them over the years, like crying at age 12 when she saw her newborn nephew Jeff because she thought he was "ugly." She'd forget something from a few minutes ago (a phone call) or last week (going out for Mexican food) or last year (three home school consultations) or from early in our marriage (my going to band practice on her birthday and again the day David came home from the hospital: I was a slow learner). She even forgot that the previous year I'd been gone most of a week to go to Texas to buy a Toyota from her family. That scared me.

Susan had always been an excellent driver with a perfect record and a mind like a GPS; but, she started having occasional trouble in planning a route from one place to another. She once had to take a detour back from her dentist due to construction and got as far Sylacauga (home of Jim Nabors: "Gomer Pyle") before she realized she was lost. That scared me more. And, things continued to gradually worsen. It got harder for her to write things as her attention and spelling were slightly off and her penmanship less legible. Reading became less enjoyable as she had to stop and decode too much phonetically. She often did not recall something forgotten even when reminded. I got even more afraid and we really started to pursue this even more vigorously. She'd had a normal EEG in 1995 and an MRI within normal limits in 1998, although it'd shown some age normal atrophy, as well as the scarring from her closed head trauma at age 21. I'd already taken a more active role in David's homeschooling and in handling our household bills and finances, although she was still driving o.k., shopping and cooking and taking care of all the rest of us. But, it looked like this was all changing and we didn't know why.

In 1998 we went to our first neurologist, who did another EEG and MRI and ran as many tests as we could think of, including some real long shots I'd come upon in all my research, such as for heavy metal toxicity. The EEG was normal and the MRI wasn't horrible although it showed more atrophy and some signs of possible chronic small vessel ischemic disease, possibly related to vascular disease with her old blood pressure problems, as well as the old left temporal-parietal scarring from her attack. The lab tests were all normal. The neurologist recommended complete neuropsychological testing which we did with a friend of my brother (who also happened to be a superb blues harmonica player, which added to his credibility in my eyes). His results showed impairments in working memory, visuomotor tracking, visual attention, propositional auditory comprehension, phonemic verbal fluency, immediate and delayed auditory memory, visual memory, high-load verbal learning, fine motor speed and a mess of other functions I only vaguely understood from my psychology training years earlier. They concluded she had mild dementia, probably Alzheimer's.

I wasn't totally devastated as this was exactly

what all my research and observations of Susan had led me to hypothesize over the past couple of years. I thought I could take care of her as long as was necessary if she could just continue to **know** me and **trust** me. I was apprehensive about all the things I knew I would have to learn; but, fortunately, I didn't know the half of it at that point or I might have been overwhelmed. I was particularly ignorant of how many emotional challenges I faced and all I'd have to learn about myself and handling my feelings. Susan started on Aricept, the only Alzheimer's drug available at that time, which would only help keep her on a plateau of current functioning for a longer period. It seemed to help with her cognition some, but at the price of lots of GI symptoms, especially diarrhea. Susan has always tried to play Pollyanna's "glad game" of finding something positive in any adversity. So, she was later grateful that she lost 35 pounds on this medication(a personal trainer would have been much easier). We got her into the Alzheimer's clinic at the University of Alabama at Birmingham to try to take advantage of any new, experimental treatments that might come along, and to try to help others by participating in their research programs. She got us both signed up to will our bodies, including brains, to UAB and her body donor card became one of her favorite possessions she wanted to have always with her.

In 2001 our friends Jackie and Wes got us into a records and phone consultation with a famous and somewhat unconventional neurologist in Florida. He doubted it was Alzheimer's; suggested there might be a vascular origin; and recommended a bunch of other tests, most of which were kind of alternative and quite unknown to me. And expensive. Meanwhile, her UAB neurologist had switched her to Exelon, which agreed with her guts better, and tried some other fancy brain scans, like PET and SPECT scans. Susan continued to struggle with her old back and neck pain, blood pressure flare-ups, mild cognitive decline and some new problems with constipation, fatigue, weakness and having to do things much more consciously and deliberately to compensate. She continued to complain of frequent episodes in which her vision would suddenly blur, her mouth get tingly, her anxiety increase and muscles get weak, which we continued to think were related to blood sugar and/or blood pressure. I did extensive record-keeping of blood pressure, pulse and blood sugar measurements, trying to get a handle on all this. Susan got us lined up with some local Alzheimer's support groups as she wanted us to use our experiences to at least be of some help to others: her basic, default setting (a primary reason I married her, remember).

By 2003 the neurologist and neuropsychologist were agreeing that the course of Susan's disease did not look like the typical Alzheimer's one. The neurologist toyed with the diagnosis of "fronto-temporal dementia" since there was so much emotional involvement. She was more easily stressed and agitated or anxious, more obsessive about things, more reactive, more likely to cry or get frustrated. However, this diagnosis didn't really fit the clinical picture either, especially as Susan seemed about the same in memory, abstract thinking, judgment, and **wit.** She could still write, dress herself, feed herself, and dial a phone, although she needed more and more help. I was still working full-time and taking care of her by a combination of phone calls and a few hours a day of sitter help by friends (Sabra, Nancy from my band) and a group of saintly women from our church, Grace and Truth (Linda, Marian, Alice, Micky, Rosemary). I saw more and more "episodes" in which right in the middle of doing something else, she would start making a chewing motion with her mouth open and lips smacking (sometimes in her sleep, too) and then lean over and close her eyes and clench her right hand. She'd try to talk, but couldn't, and I had only a few seconds to get her to a chair or I believed she'd fall down. She'd be minimally responsive to my directions and then later feel all wiped out for hours and not have any recall of what had happened. These only lasted a minute or so and she'd recover whether or not she had a glucose tablet and her blood sugar and blood pressure would measure normal. Finally, our daughter-in-law, Christina, reported what sounded to me like a grand mal seizure in our kitchen and I then observed an obvious grand mal seizure she had in bed while asleep. Turns out she was mostly having complex partial seizures, which I'd never heard of. She started on Depakote and we began another chapter in our adventure, with an increased need for safety and a risk of injury from falling. She had already stopped driving, primarily for vision loss.

UAB stopped taking our insurance and we started with a third neurologist her internist had recommended: a very tall and kind man, who had a beautiful singing voice and had sung in college with Bert Pitts, the psychologist I later went to work for in 2007 after we closed the practice with my twin (Bert had also gotten his psychology doctorate from Baylor and once sang at the symphony with Dave Brubeck, whom I'd modeled my college jazz quartet after...all these connections...I like the connections). At about this same time, one of my patients, Debbie C., *Blessed* Debbie C., was kindly asking me how my wife was as she always did at the beginning of her sessions. My answer led her to more questions until she told me about the disease that had almost taken her life and that Susan's clinical picture had come more and more to resemble, even though her history had not. We asked the new neurologist to do the simple blood tests for this disease, which came back positive. He diagnosed her with antiphospholipid antibody syndrome, an autoimmune disorder I also never heard of, and started her on Coumadin, a blood thinner, to stop the clotting strokes that had been ravaging her brain for years. He was clear this would not repair any existing damage but hoped it would allow a "permanent plateau" of her current functioning. A new MRI showed a lot more atrophy and lots of "microvascular changes" from these little strokes and TIA's. This neurologist took a new position at St. Vincent's Hospital (and bought a house from the couple in my band) and we ended up back again with the first neurologist we had seen and whom we continue to see.

****

Eventually Susan's need for care got way beyond what our volunteers could provide and I began having to use hired agency sitters. A couple of these didn't work out too well (one even went shopping on my nickel and told Susan not to tell) but most were very professional and extraordinarily kind. And expensive. Of course Susan "fell in love" with and "adopted" each of them. We finally got the seizures and blood pressure problems under reasonable control, with the last seizure noticed in about 2008 and her even going off blood pressure meds in 2010 or so. However, we haven't gotten the full permanent plateau we hoped for as she has had several more strokes in 2011 and 2012. She has had a number of ER trips, more brain scans and a couple of stints in a rehab hospital. These strokes resulted in her losing more use of her left hand and leg and needing even more support from someone else to do any walking or standing.

She lost some of her sense of how her limbs and body are located in space, as well as balance. And, what has been most devastating to her overall, she lost a lot of her visual processing ability. She can sort of see shapes but not usually details or colors. Her eyes still send a decent signal, even with the near- sightedness and kerataconus. But, her brain is very spotty, unpredictable and impaired about how it can process the signal. She became legally and functionally blind. She had gradually spent more and more of her time in watching TV: movies, Willie Nelson concert videos, educational material, etc. So, this was even more of a loss to her than was losing driving, reading and writing, personal mobility and autonomy, and the abilities to feed, bathe, dress, groom and toilet herself. Biggest of all has been her loss of ability to **do** things for others. Her memory has gotten slightly worse but I also have seen significant changes in her reasoning, her judgment, her concentration and her personality. Some of these are weird, like sometimes forgetting that she is so disabled in some areas, like her ability to walk or take care of herself. I also see her as more "resistant" and argumentative, which probably reflects more loss of control and independence as well as reactions to **my** behavior, which is not always great.

The emotional strain of doing psychotherapy all day with hurting couples, families and individuals and then coming home to take care of Susan with all its emotional strain, has worn me down more and more. This showed up in my being much less patient and kind and tolerant and being irritable to the point of often losing my temper and hollering. So, when I turned 65 and became Medicare eligible in 2012, I decided to retire and take care of Susan all on my own. As I write now in June of 2013 we are still very much in the transition to this new stage of our life. I have written more, played my music more, spent a lot of time reading or narrating movies to Susan and increased my running and back strength exercises. I feel less stressed overall and am generally doing a better caregiving job, although I still "lose it" too frequently, which will all be discussed in the "Caregiver Carols" in this book. But, now you know how we got where we are and what we're dealing with.

****

Who knows what we'll have to face tomorrow?

DNA: **D**ID **N**OT **A**SSESS

Verses:
As a kid she was allergic to her little cat.
But she got shots every week and that took care of that.

In her childhood low blood sugar made her weak or worse.
But she ate high protein snacks, kept glucose in her purse.

Chorus:
How does she look and can she cook and does she like to play?
Does she have cute chromosomes and sexy DNA?

Verses:
As a grownup, curving corneas made vision blurry.
But she got new contacts and pursued her usual hurry.

Then more pressure in her life: high pressure in her heart.
But, she researched pills and doctors, man, that gal is smart.

Chorus:
Yeah, it's great she looks first rate, her figure's A-O.K.
But does she have cool chromosomes and foxy DNA?

Verses:
Then the pain grew worse and worse from her arthritic disc.
No longer was she statuesque, my artsy obelisk.

She developed dermatitis on her face and head.
Now we use three weird shampoos and really gooey med.

Chorus:
Silky hair, complexion fair, funny, sweet and gay.
Did she lack keen chromosomes and lusty DNA?

Verses:
Then onto strokes that limited her memory and motion.
Did a mess of damage that you can't cure with a lotion.

With the damage to her brain she got a kind of seizure.
All this aged her terribly to prematurely "geezer."

Chorus:
Instead of dancing and romancing so frenetically,
May be I should have paused a 'sec..... and checked genetically.

She's had to bear more than her share of pains and drains and ills,
Had to see too many doctors, take too many pills.

If I had known would I have flown, turned tail and run away?
Or still fall deep in love despite deficient DNA?

    This is kind of a silly piece; but, it has occasionally occurred to me that I wish I would have known that Susan was going to have four people's share of medical problems. I knew her, and her family and family history, very well after three years of dating. We'd been through a lot together, seen each other under many different circumstances and talked ad infinitum about everything imaginable. The medical things that did run in her family, like breast cancer, bipolar disorder and diabetes, have not turned out to be any of Susan's problems anyway. DNA testing was not available back then to give some idea of high risk areas; but, my own recent DNA profile showed me highest at risk for diabetes and glaucoma, which I don't have and aren't prominent in my family history, and I'm only at average risk for the skin cancer I've already had. So, it might not have been helpful anyway. And, truth be told, I believe I would have married her in spite of all that knowledge, as it came down to love and willingness to take on whatever life would throw at us. Maybe if I'd known in the first three minutes we met since I was pretty much gone after five. I know she would have honored her commitment to take care of me if things had been reversed. Just seems sometimes like it would have been nice to give fully INFORMED consent. But, I guess nobody really gets that, so I won't resent having to honor my commitment to her (except maybe every once in a great while, just a teensy little bit). You and I also need to resist the temptation to imagine that this is all somehow our fault or punishment for being merely imperfectly human, especially with regard to our loved one we're taking care of now.

HEART-EYES
Verses:
He can still see...
How she looked so long ago, the day they both began to know,
That they'd be together, care forever and they'd never cease to love each other.
Through his memory...
She looks willowy and tall, gliding 'cross the campus mall like it's still here.

In his mind's view...
She's that vision he still sees, floating towards him with the breeze,
With her silk dress flowing, long hair blowing, soft skin glowing golden in the sunlight.
He can tell you...
Of the sweetness in her face, as her slender arms embrace and draw him near.

Chorus:
So it isn't that his vision's weak and fuzzy,
Or it's clouded by a past he's dreaming of.
He both sees her as she **was** and **is** because he
Always sees her through the heart-eyes of his love.

Verses:
Yet he knows well...
Every roll and every wrinkle, every fold and every crinkle,
How some parts are bagging, others sagging, time is dragging down her youthful beauty.
He can still tell...
Gravity has taken toll, even on this loving soul he calls his own.

He sees clearly...
Where there's now a bulging spot, now a blemish, scar or blot,
Where the skin is stretched, lines are etched, changes fetched by time's relentless pull.
And sincerely...

He perceives her how she is: a real woman who is his and his alone.

Chorus:
So it isn't that his vision's weak and fuzzy,
Or it's clouded by a past he's dreaming of.
*He both sees her as she **was** and **is** because he*
Always sees her through the heart-eyes of his love.

    I've had many people tell me they can simultaneously see their spouse exactly as they really are in the present as well as how they looked many years ago when they first fell in love. After over 45 years of relationship with Susan, I now believe them and know what they mean. As we get older we can, and should I guess, develop **"double vision."** This applies literally to our spouse's physical appearance, but metaphorically, too, to speak about changes that may have occurred in abilities or even personality, through aging, illness, dementia or injury. Susan has become very different through her strokes and years of being disabled, dependent and depressed. She hasn't greyed or wrinkled nearly as much as many people her age, which helps; but, the wear and tear on her from her condition does show, both physically and psychologically. Yet, I can still see her as the old Susan, even if I have to consciously work at it sometimes. Something seems a little weird to me about wanting to be intimate with an aging, disabled, debilitated body and I sometimes wonder what other people think about it, which embarrasses me. I know her body looks very different from how it did in the early 70's (so does mine); but, overall, I guess I think it's cool I can still get turned on by it and enjoy sharing some happiness together. And it's even nicer she's still mostly the person I've loved, respected and related to since 1968.

    My early emotional adjustment was mostly to the *idea* of the diagnosis of Alzheimer's and what I anticipated that would mean for me and for her over the coming years. At first she wasn't all that different in behavior or abilities or personality. She still drove, cooked, managed the kids, called people, etc., etc. But, I was very afraid of what might happen as the disease progressed, both for my caregiving responsibilities and for our relationship. I remember sitting with our friends Sabra (Susan's first friend in Birmingham she met in 1976) and Dan (he turned me on to Bob Marley's reggae) at Dave's Pizza, where I sometimes played with another bluegrass band. I told them tearfully that I thought maybe I could take care of Susan forever if she just would always **know** me and **trust** me. That was my deepest hope and prayer and it has mostly been fulfilled, maybe in part as her mild dementia is vascular instead of Alzheimer's, although the trust half of the equation has sometimes been strained to the max. And, I still try to look at her through my "heart-eyes." I definitely want to encourage you to look at the loved one you're caring for through your heart-eyes. Don't deny or ignore the problems or reasons why you're caring for them; but, keep in mind the image and memory of what made them become your "loved" one in the first place.

I CAN DO IT ALL

Verses:
Do you need some help with feeding?
No, I think I'm good.
Can you cope if she starts bleeding?
Yes, I think I could.

Do you need some help with dressing?
Thanks, I think I'm fine.
Other needs that need addressing?
I don't want to whine.

Chorus:
Sure, I can run a marathon; I'll start one right away.
Uphill? Backwards? In the dark? Just point out the way.
Through a hailstorm? Straight-line winds? I will never fall.
Toting someone on my back? Hey, I can do it all!

Verses:
Can you keep up with your own work?
Yes, but thanks for asking.
Are there chores you'll have to shirk?
I'm great at multi-tasking.

Can I help you with the mopping?
I'll do it 'fore long.
What if she starts into flopping?
I stay pretty strong.

Chorus:
Sure, I can climb Mt. Everest; I'll start out right away.
Hopping? Backwards? In the dark? Just point out the way.
Through a snowstorm? 'Cross a glacier? I will never fall.
Toting someone on my back? Hey, I can do it all!

Verses:
Does her hair need brushing, combing?
Hey, I've got the knack.
What if she's confused and roaming?
I'll just fetch her back.

Do you have too many dishes?
No more than most others.
Will you give her all her wishes?
If I have my druthers.

Chorus:
Sure, I can swim the English Channel; I'll start right away.
Underwater? In the dark? Just point out the way.
Through a windstorm? In a typhoon? I will never stall.
Toting someone on my back? Hey, I can do it all!

I thought that I could do it all: "Bring it on" I said.
I thought that I would never stall: "See, I'm still not dead."
"Shrink, musician, runner, father, why not be a 'carer'?"
One of many thoughts I thought that proved to be in error.

    This is where I started out in the caregiving business and, for a while, it was realistic...sort of. I wanted to take care of Susan myself, do a good job and learn how to do whatever needed doing. I like to feel competent and self-sufficient. I value being kind and serving others: I think it's why we're here. I thought I could handle it all and so far, I can...sort of. I wanted to protect my family and friends from having to be involved in taking care of her as much as possible. I had the idea I needed to save them for later when it "really gets rough," even though I probably denied them some good feelings from helping someone else. I also thought it was *easier* to just do it myself than having to teach someone else to do things I already knew how to do, mostly from trial and error, especially error.

    I appreciate the kindness and loving care behind the offers; but, I think the responsibility is mine and I feel guilty having others do too much of my job. It can feel like I'm shirking my duty. I think that because I know her so well and have done so much caregiving that I really can do it better than anyone else. I also have a vague sense that I don't deserve the assistance and didn't earn it or I have to pay them or do something in return or that I now am in debt to them. Wow, lots of complicated emotions.

Truth is, I'm also not very good at asking for help. I'm used to being the *helper,* not the *helpee.* Plus, I'm shy. I guess I am also a bit prideful in thinking I can do it better and so, it has to be done my "better" way. O.K., I want to be in control, too, and get the occasional mileage out of being the hero, saint or martyr. But, I'm afraid there may also be the factor of my not wanting to fully accept how difficult and all-consuming my job is or how much help I really need or how much it's likely to get worse in the future. So, if I don't actually have body parts falling off or decaying, I tell myself things are all right. But, I do think there's a high probability she will have more strokes and we both are only getting older (even if I don't *feel* older). I don't want to be like the frog in the frying pan who doesn't notice the temperature very gradually getting higher until he's toast. And, I have to admit, it is very restorative to have times I can relax my body and mind because I know someone caring is caring for my caregivee. That was one nice thing about work before I retired. I **can't** do it all. It wouldn't be good for me to do it all. And, I do need some help. And, at some point, you will most likely need help from others, too. Give other people the gift of giving to you.

Like me, you may also have to examine some of your thoughts and beliefs about yourself and what is right and responsible. You may have to modify some or even give some others up. For example, I have always thought that if I **can** do something myself, then I **should** do it myself: it's MY responsibility. Similarly, I thought that being fiscally responsible meant that I should do what I can do myself rather than paying someone else to do it. That belief made a lot of sense when I was younger, and poorer, too. But, at some point in my caregiving I needed to change that to fit the times and my need for help and rest. So, what are *you* thinking and believing that you need to question and maybe change related to your caregiving? Are you holding onto some things out of pride or stubbornness or lack of awareness or an image of yourself you're protecting or anxiety about changing? It doesn't have to be done perfectly or even the "best" it can (who knows what those even mean) and no one is sitting there with a clipboard grading you or judging you and announcing the results to the world. Sometimes friends or other family members or even your caregivee can see things when you can't. So....ASK them.

It occurs to me that this may also be true at times about your seeing or not seeing the changes in needs or abilities of your caregivee. We tend to see what we're expecting to see or are accustomed to seeing and it would be easy to miss an important new development. We all probably need periodic feedback from someone outside ourselves to show us what we are missing. So...ASK them.

TOO MUCH TO THINK

Verses:
Don't forget to get her pads, her pain patch, and her pills.
Don't forget to call her dentist, pay her doctors' bills.

Remember to turn on a movie, leave her out a snack.
Remember to check in at noon, get lotion for her back.

Chorus:
My mind is whirling round and round, like skaters in a rink
And last night I had too much to think.

Verses:
Don't forget to tell her David called or she'll get stoked.
Don't forget to file her nails tonight or I'll get poked!

Remember to put out the light, turn on her heating pad.
Remember to clean towels and sheets: she's likely to get mad.

Chorus:
I must retain it in my brain, I'm scared my skull will shrink
And last night I had too much to think.

Verses:
Don't forget to double diaper, empty out her potty.
Don't forget what I forgot, I fear I'm getting dotty.

Remember not to make the bobby pins or laces tight.
Remember to use just the small spoon, leave the juice in sight.

Chorus:
My head is spinning fast and I'm not feeling in the pink,
My brain is always on the edge: it teeters on the brink,
My mind is full of everything except the kitchen sink,
When I recall it all it almost makes me want to drink,
But tonight I'll have too much to think.

    The title and hook line for this selection were inspired by the name of a column in *Black & White*, Birmingham's city newspaper. Being a caregiver has meant an ever- growing list of additional things I have to **do** every day. After all, I'm basically handling all the daily tasks for **two** people to live their lives. However, the straining and draining part of all this has been more the thought involved in caregiving. The doing is physically tiring; but, I still have a lot of energy and usually don't mind the extra chores so much. However, the planning, deciding, analyzing, remembering, re-examining, monitoring, i.e. the **thinking**, are emotionally depleting and often overwhelming for me. Sometimes it's actually refreshing to just get immersed in some task where it's mindless, a known entity, repetitive, monotonous and just requires **doing.** I get aggravated with myself because I'm constantly forgetting to do something. Even if I make lists, I sometimes forget to look at the list! There are just millions of little details I have to keep in mind: pull the sock tight or it'll hurt her heal; get the smaller spoon or the bites will feel too big for her; check to see that her elbows are on the armrest of the wheelchair or she'll bump them on the door frame; get a pain patch for her neck before we start the morning cleanup; get some tissue for her eyes ready for when I give her the nightly eyedrops; monitor how long it's been since her last snack; etc., etc., etc., etc., etc., etc. Plus, it's a lot like having a toddler, where a little portion of your brain has to be constantly thinking about what she's doing, what does she need, is she o.k., and so forth and so on. Wow, it's no wonder I think too much: I have too much to think!

Sound familiar? I'll just bet you have too much to think, too. Can you let some other folks do some of the thinking sometimes and can you find a way to let your mind rest and not think or maybe think differently for awhile? You might consider learning about meditation or having an empty mind (e.g. check out Tara Brach's materials). Prayer is very helpful for many people. I find I can give my brain more peace when I am running and just watch the trees and birds go by. Playing a musical instrument lets my mind be focused elsewhere for a time as I can't think about caregiving and what scale to play over an F#m chord at the same time. Can you find something (woodworking, shooting pool, painting, cooking, reading, watching something on TV that's really dumb, etc.) that will hold your attention or inattention away from your caregiving so you can have a break from too much to think?

CAREGIVING HERO

Verses:
I dahwannabe a caregiving hero, just wanna be a slob.
Wanna cruise along at bare-living zero, just wanna be a blob.

I dahwannabe an inspiration, just wannna suck my thumb.
Wanna take me on a long vacation, just wanna beach my bum.

Chorus:
Caregiving takes care of all my nights and days,
I look heroic mostly 'cause I fake it.
Want a job with accolades and glory, honor, praise?
I'd give it where and when you'd care to take it.

Verses:
I dahwannabe a caregiving saint--NO--just wanna be a sap.
Wanna schlep along with no constraint so, I can just take a nap.

I dahwannabe a caregiving hero, just wanna be retired.
Wanna fiddle like a Rome-burning Nero, just wanna get fired.

Chorus:
Caregiving brings out a ton of tears and fears,
I look so brave but doubt that I can make it.
Want a job with compliments and admiration, cheers?
I'd give it where and when you'd care to take it.

  These lyrics were inspired by Bruce, a former client of mine whom I do regard as a caregiving hero. He is staying with and taking care of his wife who is seriously afflicted by physical and mental disorders, despite having extremely debilitating, painful and potentially life-threatening medical problems of his own. People often tell him he is a hero and an inspiration. I agree with them. But, he is weary and would like very much not to have to be so heroic. If he could just get around his beliefs, values, commitments and integrity. I understand him.

  Like Bruce, I am often told how much someone

respects, admires and is moved by my dedicated, persistent caregiving of Susan that I manage to do with some degree of perspective, kindness, humor and positive attitude. I have to admit that I often love to hear this praise and sympathy and bathe in the compassionate, understanding and caring feelings they come from. I need them and rely on them, I think. However, I also feel a guilty fraud as these people don't know how mean, ugly, petty and nasty I can speak to Susan when I'm really mad. They don't know of my morbid daydreams about what could happen that would relieve me of my "heroic" responsibilities, as I sing of in "Eyes on Demise." Moreover, I don't want the risks of being a hero on a pedestal or becoming a martyr. When you're on a pedestal you can't take a step in any direction or you'll fall off. And, you can't hug anyone; your neck hurts looking down all the time; and it's just a matter of time until you fall. Only way to go is down. As to martyrs: no one invites them to parties as they just make the rest of us feel guilty or manipulated. Martyrs are mostly fun for slowly torturing and putting to death. No thanks.

It's probably selfish of me to hog all this hero's glory. Maybe someone else would like a turn? But, I recommend you don't let anyone put you on a pedestal or give you a hero medal. Even if you could live up to it, you don't need to try.

CAREGIVING BURNOUT

Verses:
I dahwannabe a caregiving burnout, don't wanna go nuts.
Wanna be a bold and dare-living spurn-doubt, hold onto my guts.
I dahwannabe a caregiving burnout, watch my "get-up-go" leave.
Wanna rest and sit my caregiving turn out, be blessed to receive.

Chorus:
Caregiving saps me more than anyone deserves.
It's the hardest task I can remember.
What if I deplete all of my critical reserves?
I don't want to be a dying ember.

Verses:
I dahwannabe be a caregiving burnout, put compassion to the test.
Wanna break before my caregiving gives out, need-a take-a little rest.

I dahwannabe a caregiving flop--NO--just wanna do right.
Wanna keep going on, never stop--SO-- just need-a hold tight.

Chorus:
Caregiving makes me feel, like a bulb that's dimming.
Rarely do I feel I'm glowing bright.
Maybe I'm a lamp wick someone is trimming.
I don't wanna burn out like a light.

Verse:
I dahwannabe a caregiving stern lout, don't wanna be a louse.
Wanna always care, always give a durn 'bout, taking care of my spouse.

Chorus:
Caregiving draws and drains out all my energy.
It wears me down so much it isn't funny.

I can't become a burned out battery.

I wannabe the Energizer Bunny.

Another danger for us caregiving "heroes" is burning out. The first thing they tell you when you become a caregiver is that you have to take care of yourself first and foremost or you burn out and become useless for your caregivee. Caregiving can be a huge physical, mental and emotional drain. It seems like there is always some decision to make, some task to do, some responsibility to think about, some emotion of your loved one to help with and some emotion of your own to struggle with. It takes enormous perseverance, self-awareness, self-control, patience and courage to go on doing all this month after month or even year after year. That just flat dab wears you out and you've got to have numerous ways to recharge your batteries. You have to learn your limits, how to ask for help and how to accept the help others offer. There's so much learning and thinking and goofing and growing to be done. And, unfortunately, most of the respites and assistance you get also require a lot of planning, action and energy on your part. They may additionally involve some emotional wrestling, ambivalence or even guilt at putting someone else out or "abandoning" your obligations to your loved one. Your care recipient may even tell you they feel mistreated by your taking care of yourself, depending on their own condition.

But, caregiving burnout is a very, very real thing and it has to be taken very, very seriously. I finally retired from my full-time practice as a psychologist and marriage and family therapist about 16 years into this, as the *emotional* strain and drain of doing both led to me being less and less caring in my caring. I could do all the doing, as long as I ignored the yard work and house repairs, but the thinking and feeling was burning me out. As I write, it's 11 months into retirement and I think it was a good decision. I also rewarded myself with a retirement gift of a beautiful

Collings mt mandola (the mandola is to the mandolin what the viola is to the violin; tuned down a fifth to c-g-d-a), increased my running to almost a daily outing (at least until I hurt my leg), self-published my first book *(LOVE LYRICS: THE MUSICAL MARITAL MANUAL)* and renewed my writing of these lyrics: all ways to have some diversion, things to look forward to and recharging for my caregiving batteries. I hope you're finding ways to recharge your batteries: it's the loving, caring thing to do for everyone concerned. Go sit down right this second and make a list of what you're doing and going to do for yourself so you won't get caregiver burnout. Then pat yourself on the back for 5 minutes and remind yourself you are a good person and you are doing an enormously tough thing. Good for you. Good for you. Now, go sit down and don't do or think ANYTHING for the next 5 minutes: you deserve it. **Tell** yourself you deserve it and mean it and believe it. I do.

GIMMICKS IN LIMERICKS

There was a caregiving musician,
Whose band aroused much opposition:
To quit was abhorrent,
To play was discordant,
Poor singing, hand-wringing musician.

There was a caregiving grandpappy,
With grandkids he's crazy and sappy.
The children, he'd find,
Would recharge his mind,
Poor childlike with wild tyke grandpappy.

There was a caregiving songwriter,
Whose tunes would depress, not delight her.
But when things went wrong,
In his mind burst a song,
Poor bluesy, renewsy songwriter.

There once was a caregiving punster,
Who sought to still be his wife's funster.
'Though she peed when she laughed,
He still practiced his craft,
Poor diapering, wipe-her-ing punster.

There once was a caregiving lover,
Whose wife, he was pleased to discover,
Still stirred both their hearts,
When she fondled his parts,
Poor touch-greedy, much-needy lover.

There once was a caregiving runner,
But she thought he ran just to shun her.
'Though he ran to be healthy,
She took it as stealthy,
Poor rundown-by-sundowny runner.

There once was a caregiving runner,
Whose exercise made him much funner.
For a jog, he would find,

*Could unclog his mind,
Poor brain-speeding, rest-needing runner.*

*There was a caregiving caregiver,
Who feared that he'd need a spare liver.
When he'd too much to think,
He'd want too much to drink,
This poor loopy, droopy caregiver.*

*There once was a caregiving shrink,
Who was scared he'd turn too much to drink.
He drank one ale a night,
Not enough to get tight,
Poor bare living, caregiving shrink.*

The point of all this is to reinforce that basic and excellent advice given to new caregivers that they have to find ways to **take care of themselves**: to give themselves some peace, some battery recharging, some nurturing, some rest, some solace and solitude, some enjoyment. Otherwise, they become useless for themselves and as caregivers for their loved one. They burnout. Of course, these lyrics are also to be able to use a limerick format (rhyme pattern: a, a, b, b, a) which I've always found appealing. Ahhh, another little *self-care* moment! I'm learning to look for those small ways to take care of myself in everything I do. It's especially nice if I can spot one in the middle of something I have to do anyway for caregiving. For example, I enjoy running errands now, as it gives me time by myself in the car to listen to what I want or think without interruptions. Writing this book, and my previous book, *Love Lyrics: The Musical Marital Manual*, has been another "gimmick" for taking care of myself. It gives me something positive to think of, be creative with and gain pleasure from and I have new ideas pop into my head when I'm cooking, running, lying in bed, showering or doing something for Susan. It's a refreshing default setting my brain can slip into. It's a little respite or mini- vacation I can skip off to. I also find it helpful in looking into my own emotions and thinking, as I learn a lot about myself and my caregiving. The focus on humor in all I do also helps me to keep some sense of perspective. Feed your sense of humor.

    The difficulty with all these self-care tools is that they often require additional effort, planning and personal cost on my part at the same time: lining up and training sitters, preparing her meals and pills and diapers and everything else she'll need, setting her up with something to watch on TV, etc., etc. Sometimes they even demand extra expense, like in hiring sitters if I will be gone long enough. I also have to contend with Susan's reactions to my doing my thing. She may feel alone or ignored or abandoned or scared if left by herself too much or even if I just go back to my "man cave" to practice an instrument. She gets jealous of my time with band mates or friends, envious of my being able to play with the grandkids and reminded of all she can't do. I may have to feel guilty for being "selfish" or choosing my thing over something she wants at the time, or my having a fuller life when hers is so bleak. I may have to listen to her obsessing anxiously for several days until an anticipated event of mine occurs, especially if it involves a stressful change for her. Some of what I do, like my running or walking, is actually good for both of us: excellent for my health and an effective anti-depressant (there is research backing up this claim) as well as keeping me strong enough to manage her. Some other things I'd really, **really** like become pretty much out of reach, like a week by myself in the Smoky Mountains or even a day by myself in my own house to listen to my most obnoxious music at full volume or watch the most inane videos I have.

You may notice I mentioned drinking a lot here and elsewhere. I thoroughly enjoy my one evening ale and have no intention of giving it up. It's a little treat I reward myself with for making it through most of another day, although I still have supper, dishes, her pills and preparing Susan for bed left to do. The alcohol is comforting and relaxing and just feels cozy and I love the taste. But, I have to be very careful about it. I have huge genetic loading for alcoholism on my mother's side and, especially when I'm stressed, I can often hear that ale calling me from the bottom bin in the fridge, even when I'm at the other end of the house. It tells me all the totally rational, beneficial reasons why it'd be o.k. to have some more ale, just tonight: "You're tired; you've worked hard; just one more won't hurt; you deserve it; you have to do nice things to take care of yourself, etc. etc."

Since the time I had kids, I've had rigid rules for myself about drinking, as I did not want to go the way of many of my relatives, with the commitment to myself that I would give it up entirely if I broke my rules. And I don't want to have to give it up. I like it and I think it helps me as another little thing I enjoy that gives me a little emotional comfort. But, there's another issue with the alcohol: it lowers inhibitions for me, like it does for everyone else. You'll notice in several of my lyrics here that I already regret not having more control over my angry reactivity and harsh mouth. I think I am probably a little more easily irritated and more prone to saying something ugly when I just have one extra ale. Remember, that's also in the evening when Susan and I are both tired anyway with her "sundowning" and my day of caregiving. So, why would I want to push that? Maybe I could work on telling the ale to "shut up" instead of Susan?

I guess the moral here for you is to find things to take care of yourself, but be aware that some of these may present difficulties or dangers in themselves. Decide about your self-care gimmicks in advance, not at the moment you're exhausted or needy. Use your good judgment and values and don't nurture yourself into some other problem. I suspect you've got enough problems already.

ONE BITE AT A TIME

Verses:
Mop the kitchen, sweep the floors, dust mites must not thrive,
Vacuum all the dirt and grit and grime.
Clean the toilet, scrub the sink, daily I must strive,
To root out all the bathroom mold and slime.

Give her water, give her food, help my wife to thrive,
Make sure all her pills get served on time.
I'm staked out on an anthill and they're eating me alive,
One mini-mouthful at a time.

Chorus:
"It ain't the 'eavy 'auling what 'urts the 'orses' 'ooves,
But the 'ammer, 'ammer, ammer' on the 'ard 'ighway."
It ain't the tough and painful stuff that carves my forehead grooves,
But all the little things I have to do and feel each day.

Verses:
The litany of memories lost, she daily does revive,
A thousand little steps I have to climb.
Tiny gripes and tiny snipes: these I must survive,
Itsy-bitsy insults quite sublime.

Little slights and mini-fights, **my** needs she'll deprive,
A daily dose of misdemeanor crime.
I'm slogging through the swamp with skeeters eating me alive,
One puny pinprick at a time.

Chorus:
"It ain't the 'eavy 'auling what 'urts the 'orses' 'ooves,
But the 'ammer, 'ammer, ammer' on the 'ard 'ighway."
It ain't the tough and painful stuff that carves my forehead grooves,
But all the little things I have to do and feel each day.

The " 'eavy 'auling" saying is one my father used to recite, that pokes fun at the British accent that likes to leave off "h's" everywhere (Henry Higgins makes the same point to Colonel Pickering in "My Fair Lady:" "Hear them down in Soho Square, dropping "h's" everywhere, speaking English any way they like."). But, the " 'urting 'orse 'ooves" metaphor also nicely expresses how I feel much of the time. I can handle the big, really difficult tasks and adjustments, the "eavy auling," while the daily barrage of little things I have to do or think or feel wear me down like the 'ammer, 'ammer,' ammer." Or, it's like the old "Chinese water torture" that wears you down by one drop at a time dripping on your forehead, until you break or at least it gets "grooved." Every day there are all the little tasks anyone has in keeping house and maintaining life, while also making a million mini-treks for more pads, emptying the potty, refilling the water bottle, getting her lip gloss, fixing a snack, fetching another tissue, etc., etc. . . .*drip* . . .*drip* . . .*drip* . . .*drip* . . .Every day there are a million mini-strains on my patience and endurance in having to respond, *AGAIN,* to her guesses about how old she is, when her next appointment is, when the videos are due at the library or her complaints the vent is blowing on her, or she's sitting on her spine, or the TV is too loud, or the bites are too big, etc.,etc.,etc. . . .*drop* . . . *drop* . . . *drop* . . .*drop* . . .You know this feeling?

I'm tied up with this water torture, drowning me alive,
One dinky droplet at a time.

But, just like the cumulative effect of all these little negative things can get to us, sometimes without our fully realizing it, we can learn to produce a healthy, life-giving effect, too, by **summing up lots of little positive things**. It involves looking for the good in every moment or occurrence, consciously letting ourselves be aware of that and taking a few seconds to savor the pleasant emotions that come along. Researchers in neuroscience believe that we can actually change the connections in our brain such that seeing the positive becomes a strong tendency, just as we humans have always had an adaptive survival tendency to spot potentially harmful things. You can apply this idea to your own positive self-care and self-affirmation by being aware of the good around and in you and how you are doing healthy things to take care of yourself. You have to make a point of **telling** yourself this and **taking a few seconds to feel** good about it: "Good for you, Don, you played your mandolin a few minutes and found a new lick to use on Gary's new song." "Alright, Don. You noticed how Susan was giving a little extra support to our neighbor about her new hairdo and you experienced some of those old 'bits of bark and stone and tin.'" Check out Rick Hanson's book, *Hardwiring Happiness* for a complete description of how to do this.

"COFFEE AND A PEACE OF I, PLEASE"

Verses:
Why do you resist me when I steer you when you walk?
Why do you insist on mumbling every time you talk?

You bellyache if I just give a little sigh or frown
When you make me get back up as soon as I've sat down.

Chorus:
I'd rather trip and split my lip and have my trousers tear in two,
Than have a brawl and daily squall, trying to take care of you.

Verses:
Why do you resist me when I wipe food from your face?
Why do you insist on grumbling, get down on my case?

You sneer and snipe if I just say a silly, small complaint
When you gripe on 'bout all I've done and everything I ain't.

Chorus:
I'd rather stay up Arctic way, herding herds of caribou,
Than have a fray most every day, trying to take care of you.

Verses:
Why do you resist me when I give your neck some rest?
Why do you insist on bending chin down onto chest?

You go on accusing that I "only want to boss you"
When you are refusing to stay still so I can floss you.

Chorus:
I'd rather crawl around a mall, with senior gals whose hair is blue,
Then have a nasty fight each night, trying to take care of you.

Verses:
Why do you resist me when I lift your arm to dress you?
Why do you insist I'm "never wrong" just to impress you?

You seem to take delight in noting each of my mistakes,

When you could make it right by helping, that is all it takes.

Chorus:
I'd rather snare a grizzly bear: that's dumb and pretty scary, too,
Then wage a war and rant and roar, trying to take care of you.

  This has been one of my toughest, ongoing struggles and I still don't have enough personal peace about it. And, I still get mad at her frequently when my first reaction is that, ONCE AGAIN, I'm having to FIGHT her in order to help her. That just isn't right! If I can slow down and think, I know she's doing the best she can, that being so disabled is tough and lots of it is new to her, too; that she gets anxious and just freezes up; that she is exhausted much of the time; that she wants and needs to maintain some sense of autonomy and that my fussing and cussing only makes it worse. There are even times when her "resistance" may be a healthy self-validation or way to have some influence with me, albeit a bit passive-aggressive (what else has she got). But, I still shoot my mouth off real fast because, damn it all, IT FEELS LIKE SHE'S "RESISTING." It seems so obvious to me she could make it so much easier for both of us if she'd "just" stand up straight, listen to my directions, relax her neck or hands or arms, think before she asks me a question or tells me a need, etc., etc., etc. I often can't tell what is something she "can't do" versus something she "won't do." And, it seems to be a moving target, as she may do something just fine in the morning (e.g. stand up straight while I clean her up) and act unable to do the same thing later in the day. That FEELS LIKE SHE'S RESISTING.

  What helps most is trying to explain **everything** to myself as coming from her disability, to make that my cognitive default setting rather than she's resisting, she's stubborn or willful, that she's Scottish, etc. I have to slow down and think, which is so much tougher for me to do than to say. This is her first time to be a caregivee, too, and she's just trying to find her way as I'm trying to find mine. It helps to remind myself that she's never been resistant or malicious in the 45 years I've known her and that I married her in the first place because she was the kindest, most caring, most accepting, best- intentioned and most generous person I'd ever met (plus being the prettiest). Fortunately, she was, and still is, one of the most forgiving people I've known, too.

You know, I was a psychotherapist for 40 years and dealt effectively with resistance every day: goes with the territory. I got tons of training in how to deal with resistance: that you don't fight it; you go with the flow; you try to understand it and you look for how you may be a part of their problem or "resistance." People don't usually see themselves as "resistant" or want to be that way. They resist for reasons that may not make sense yet to you, but probably make good sense to them and they need help to get around it. But, I often haven't tapped into that insight or skill with Susan and frequently don't come at it with all that great understanding I just talked about. So, I wonder if I'm seeing her as "resistant" because it's easier to accept than fully realizing just how damaged and disabled she truly is? I know how to deal with "I won't" lots better than with "I can't." Am I the one who's really resistant? Is your caregivee "resistant" or just making what to them seems a reasonable or best possible response to their condition or to you?

'UMBLE

Her walk is a stumble, her speech is a mumble, her grasp is a fumble, her standing a tumble.

Her thoughts are a jumble, her words are a bumble, her posture a crumble, her bowels a rumble.

*But, her courage is strong and it's rare that she'll grumble
My courage is weak and I gripe...and feel humble.*

    This is pretty self-explanatory but I'll comment a bit. I'm occasionally very struck by how hard Susan's life is and how she bears up under it. I seriously doubt I could do as well if our situations were reversed (although I've thrown it up to her in my anger that I could). She's been dealing with the progressive loss of ability and life quality for fifteen years now. That's a long time. Her motto has always been **"bloom where you're planted"** and she's always tried to find something positive to be appreciative of in any adversity. Like Pollyanna (watch the Masterpiece Theatre version), she tries to play the "glad game" the best she can, although it's getting harder and harder.

    I, on the other hand, believe in and try to do the same, but find myself falling way short of my ideals over and over. For example: in the middle of my typing this out just now Susan asked me to hand her the tissue she can't secure for herself. In the process, she knocked over the vase of roses our sweet neighbors, Blake and Erin, brought her for Mothers Day, despite my directions, cautions and finally yelling "stop, stop." My reaction was to cuss and fuss that she didn't listen and made a mess, even though the mess was on her, not me, and was only water to begin with. I felt sorry for myself being interrupted and having to clean up the spill, while she apologized profusely. I felt kinda' stupid and ashamed: dumbled and humbled.

It's a shame that Pollyanna's "glad game" has been dismissed as naive, shallow, juvenile and, well: "Pollyannish." There's a lot to be said for developing the habit or attitude of being positive and trying to find some good in everything. As I did in my first book, I'd like to quote Charles Swindoll for you:

The remarkable thing is we have a choice every day regarding the attitude we will embrace for that day. We cannot change our past...We cannot change the fact that people will act in a certain way. We cannot change the inevitable. The only thing we can do is play on the one string we have, and that is our attitude...I am convinced that life is 10% what happens to me and 90% how I react to it. And so it is with you . . . We are in charge of our Attitudes.

And I feel "'umble" that disabled old Susan is still better at it than I am.

PREDICTABLY UNPREDICTABLE

Verses:
Sometimes she can stand alone, not need support at all.
Other times if I don't help, she'd just collapse and fall.
Sometimes she can pop right up and stand up tall and straight.
Other times her back stays bent and I hold all her weight.

Sometimes she can walk o.k., not needing my assistance.
Other times she's stuck in mud and slogging through resistance.
Sometimes she can keep her balance, move her legs real neat.
Other times she leans and sways as I direct her feet.

Chorus:
Why can't she consistently, be the same, not vary?
Why does she change constantly; I find it very scary?
I never know what to expect, I'm always being tricked.
I never can predict her and that's why I stay ticked.

Verses:
Sometimes her remembering just really fires and works.
Other times it's like a car that stops and starts and jerks.
Sometimes a memory gets fixed, she'll easily replay it.
Other times it will not stick, no matter how I say it.

Sometimes her recall is strong, not foggy, dim or hazy.
Other times it all is wrong; it really drives me crazy.
Sometimes I can stake my life on what she's recollecting.
Other times I take my wife's report as needing checking.

Chorus:
Why can't she consistently, be the same, not vary?
Why does she change constantly; I find it very scary?
I never know what to expect, I'm frequently outslicked.
I never can predict her and that's why I stay ticked.

Verses:
Sometimes she can't tell if I hold up a mop or broom.
Other times she'll read my face from clear across the room.
Sometimes she can't say which actor's face is on TV.
Other times she'll spot an antique plate I barely see.

Chorus:
Why can't she consistently, be the same, not vary?
Why does she change constantly; I find it very scary?
I never know what to expect, my knickers all get nicked.
I never can predict her and that's why I stay ticked.

Verses:
Sometimes she can cope quite well: her spirit's strong and soaring.
Other times her life is hell and wrong and dumb and boring.
Sometimes she'll be positive and optimistic, too.
Other times it's doom and gloom and blackness through and through.

Chorus:
Why can't she consistently, be the same, not vary?
Why does she change constantly; I find it very scary?
I never know what to expect, my butt keeps getting kicked.
I never can predict her and that's why I stay ticked.

    Most of us want to have some control over what happens to us in life and it sure does help with that if we have some sense about what's coming next. I'm generally fairly decent at going with the flow and adapting to what I need to. I think I have a reasonably good confidence in my own ability to figure out what I have to do or get someone else involved in helping when that becomes necessary. But, I also put too high a premium on being right, looking good, seeming knowledgeable, doing things exceptionally well and being competent and versatile in a very wide range of areas. Most people would probably say I'm really on top of things, patient, easy-going and flexible. However, my grandmother's maiden name was Blume and Grandpa Wendorf always said that at least Blume ladies (i.e. Grandma and her sisters, Great Grandma, etc.) were all chronically anxious: "Nervous Nellies" he called them. I think I inherited a base level of anxiety higher than the average and particularly in terms of shyness and social anxiety. After working on this for 66 years, I'm usually good at managing it, and have learned to disregard my initial anxiety as a "false alarm" where there really is no danger (it doesn't make all the anxiety vanish but able to be tolerated until I calm down). However, caregiving has really stretched and stressed me and my anxiety, while pushing me to learn and grow even more and in more areas. I'm doing it, but it can come at a price. Sometimes that price shows up in annoyance, irritability, aggravation, impatience and even anger. I know that a lot of this comes with the caregiving territory, but I don't like it and I get tired of trying harder, screwing up again, apologizing and trying to forgive myself over and over. I can count only on Susan's situation constantly changing; so, I stay off balance and often just get ticked. Anxiety in either of us can show up as anger, control or complaining. Might happen with you, too? Monitoring and managing anxiety is where it's at. When in doubt, think *"What am I **ANXIOUS** about here?"*

UP THE CREEK WITHOUT A GPS

Verses:
There's in-home, assisted; there's indie care, too.
Alzheimer's, nursing; which should I pursue?

There's internal medicine, family doc's, too.
Perhaps gerontologists. I wish I knew.

I don't know your future, just what you will need.
How to decide on which way to proceed?

Chorus:
Where's my road map, my directions? Where's my GPS?
How will I know where I am going? Trial and error? Guess?
Where's a road sign? Find a landmark. What am I to do?
I'm just groping in the dark and haven't got a clue.

Bridge:
Caregiving comes without handbooks or rules,
No set of instructions, no box full of tools.
I want to choose rightly, I want to do well.
But making decisions is caregiving hell.

Verses:
Are you being stubborn or willful or scared,
Demented or prideful or simply impaired?

Are you being truthful, insisting it's so,
Forgetful or fibbing, just how can I know?

Are you really nauseous or just thinking so?
Are you really hurting or just feeling low?

Chorus:
Where's the lighthouse, where's the buoy, I can't hear the bell.
Are there navigation charts? How am I to tell?
Where are channel markers? This nighttime fog is bleak.
I'm boating with no compass and sailing up the creek.

Bridge:
Caregiving comes with no manual given,
No list of directions for caregiving living.
I want to choose wisely, I don't want to yell.
But making decisions is caregiving hell.

One of the toughest parts of caregiving for me is never being real sure what I'm doing or what I'll have to plan for in our future. I can try to predict based on what's happened in the past. I can seek and take the feedback of doctors, rehab therapists and other professionals. I can get advice from family and friends. I can ask Susan's thoughts on her condition and needs and I can observe her behavior and reactions for myself. I can experiment and learn from my mistakes. I can do online research on her condition and possible answers to each new question that arises. But, I can't **know** what to do or if I'm doing it all properly or how to prepare for what I'll have to do next. Decisions, decisions, decisions. There's never any lack of decisions, just a lack of foresight, knowledge, awareness and information. Where's my instruction manual? Where's the Help/Support number to call? Where's my GPS?

My anesthesiologist uncle used to ask my law professor father how much he **didn't** know about the law. "That," Uncle Jack would say, "is how much we doctors don't know about medicine." They'd agree: "we're just groping in the dark, all of us." I knew that feeling over forty years as a psychotherapist. I know that feeling every time I try to do anything new on my computer or phone or try to hook up something new on my TV. And, I've known it now as a caregiver since 1995. I'm a little bit tired of it. Decisions, decisions, decisions. Ambivalence, ambivalence, ambivalence. Anxiety, anxiety, anxiety.

But remember, why *should* you or I know everything

about what we're doing or will have to do down the road? We haven't done this a dozen times before and, unfortunately, we can't see into the future. We've gotten this far and we'll deal with what we have to.

We also don't have to constantly "re-invent the wheel" all by ourselves. There are more and more communities that have support groups for caregivers and there are an increasing number of online support/discussion groups and information sites. In some you can even ask questions and get answers from experts or other caregivers who have dealt with your particular concern. I found a bunch of good support groups through LinkedIn (you can even specify the problem you're dealing with) but also check out www.care-givers.com (Empowering Caregivers), www.wellspouse.org, www.agingcare.com, www.supportgroups.com, www.helpguide.org, and www.caregiver.com.

COACH TALK

Verse:
"Anything worth doing, is worth doing well."
That sounds like wise words for living.
But most of what I do doesn't need to excel,
"cause there's too much care to be giving.

Chorus:
Coach talk, coach talk: living by a platitude,
May help to motivate the team.
Coach talk, coach talk: gives me an ATTITUDE,
Makes me want to throw up and scream.

Verse:
"When the going gets tough, the tough get going."
That sounds so wise, so true.
Well wherever they go, I wish I was knowing,
'Cause I'd like to go there, too!

Chorus:
Coach talk, coach talk: living by cliche',
May help the players keep on striving.
Coach talk, coach talk: I don't want to play,
I'm now mostly 'bout just surviving.

Verse:
"Winners never quit, quitters never win."
That sounds like advice that is good.
But I don't wanna' win, this job does me in,
And I'd quit it in a minute if I could!

Chorus:
Coach talk, coach talk: living by a slogan,
May help the Samurai to fight.
Coach talk, coach talk: do I look like a Shogun?
I just wanna' make it through the night.

I'm perfectionistic and moralistic enough all on my

own. I don't need external help to demand even more of myself that is unrealistic and a setup for failure, regret and more guilt. So, I have to question the cultural expectations that push me to compare myself with the "winners" and "heroes" and "saints" of the caregiving world. I'm just me; I try hard; I do some things reasonably well; and I'm probably doing close to my best without killing myself or risking even more burnout than I already have. I resist making decisions and living my life by slogans or mindless truisms: they so often turn out to be wrong or merely half-truths. That kind of stuff may work well for motivating athletes or salesmen or soldiers, but I think we have to be careful about applying them to any and all people and situations. As caregivers, we also have to be kinder to ourselves and realize we are only human and WE WILL MAKE MISTAKES AND HAVE SOME UNPLEASANT EMOTIONS. We need to see "winning" more as doing as well as we can with the tough times we're having and still holding onto some kind, positive, caring and hopeful attitudes. If you hear yourself saying "no pain, no gain," then stomp real hard on your left foot with your right. Hurt? So, what did you gain? Pain is our body's way of telling us something needs attention. Don't go looking for it; just deal with what needs attention. Your caregiving doesn't have to be (and can't be) "perfect" (whatever in the world that means): just good enough will do fine.

PROUD OUT LOUD

Verses:
I've learned how to shop and cook and keep us fairly healthy.
While I worked and kept on earning, though we're far from wealthy.

I have figured how to dress and comb and brush and clean her,
How to wipe her, fix her diaper, doll her up and preen her.

I've become a good caregiver, should my head be bowed?
Is it o.k. to sometimes say I'm rather proud, out loud?

Chorus:
I ain't trying to be prideful,
Pride goes 'fore a fall.
Not at all do I feel snideful,
Towards the rest of y'all.

Verses:
I've always kept my running up, which keeps my poundage down.
I've learned to better handle fears, not always act the clown.

I've kept the house from condemnation, though there's rotten wood.
I've kept the inside fairly clean, though not like how I should.

I've managed pills and food and bills, her laundry and trousseau.
I don't care she did it better, forty years ago!

Chorus:
I ain't arrogant to no one,
Just part of the crowd.
I'm just proud of all I've done,
And saying it out loud.

Caregiving for me has meant a perpetual learning curve. Just as I think I'm on top of things and doing pretty well, something new comes along and brings a whole new set of challenges and things to learn. It may be a new task, like how to help Susan walk differently after another stroke that impairs her left leg control or her sense of how her body is situated in space. It may be coming up with new ways to provide her a better quality of life, like how to stay tuned in and occupied and entertained after a stroke messes up her processing of visual information, such as audio books or reading to her or narrating movies to her or giving her verbal cues when moving around ("Move your right foot a step to the left").

Often it seems the new learning involves my own personal growth and development, such as dealing with my shyness or anxiety in talking with unknown insurance people or beefing up my patience and courage in handling the fears or loss or aggravation all her changes mean for me. This has been and continues to be and will probably always be very, very, very hard, at least at times. "Pride" or more precisely, an arrogant disdainful, hubris or "Pridefulness" is said to be the most serious of the "Seven Deadly Sins" as it involves being haughty or condescending or dismissive toward others.

But, I have learned and grown and dealt with and done an awful lot and I think I'm entitled to be a little proud of it. The Father made it clear he was proud of his Son, Jesus; I'm outspokenly proud of my sons and daughters-in-law and grandchildren; and sometimes I'm proud of myself. Good parents express pride of their children and *good self-care as an adult is much like being a good parent to oneself.* It's healthy for parents to nurture, take care of, reward, forgive and show compassion to their kids, as well as to teach and discipline them.

I'm pretty good at criticizing myself for what I've done wrong or haven't done that I should. Occasionally, I think it's o.k. and healthy to verbalize it audibly: I'm proud out loud and you probably should be, too. So, say it out loud. Let me hear it.

PRIDE INSIDE

Verses:
When I'm buying ladies' diapers, must leave macho-ness outside,
Female pads or girly wipers, I can't bring in mannish pride.
I can't go all green and gooshy, when it's time for me to pay,
I'll pretend I'm buying sushi and I do this every day.

If I take her out to dinner and to take a little ride,
I can't be a prideful sinner, have to leave home foolish pride,
Try to eat my meal in leisure, although wheelchair dates ain't "cool."
Don't be scared she'll have a seizure, pull her hair or start to drool.

Chorus:
It's fine to say I've done o.k., to say I'm proud out loud,
But vanity runs deep in me, with shame I'm well endowed,
Be mortified if I am spied out with my damaged bride?
I know I've got to go and hide my foolish pride inside.

Verse:
When we go to see her doctor I'll leave pride home at our dwelling,
But I know that it'd shock her, if I died 'cause she starts smelling.
Though embarrassed I can't shirk assisting with her mammograms,
Discuss what body parts don't work, help her pelvis get exams.

Chorus:
It's fine to say I've done o.k., to say I'm proud out loud,
But vanity runs deep in me, with shame I'm well endowed,
Be mortified if I am spied out with my damaged bride?
I know I've got to go and hide my foolish pride inside.

As Susan got more impaired with strokes and seizures and it became more obvious to everyone, I struggled for awhile with feeling embarrassed at being seen with her out in public. Her gait got very shaky and she then needed the wheelchair most of the time. Her head was bent over with her arthritic neck problems; she spilled food and eventually had to be fed; and she was sometimes inappropriate in what she said and who she talked to, especially as her vision got worse and worse. I was very aware of other people looking at us and probably felt they were even when they weren't. I wanted things to stay as normal as possible for as long as possible, even when they weren't. I tried to be super casual and act like everything was fine and we were mostly like everybody else and I could take care of her while continuing to do just as I would have done before. No big deal; "it's all part of life's rich pageant;" I can do it all. Right.

But, the truth was that everything was very changed and changing more all the time. And, part of my struggle was with my own image and pride. I wanted to look o.k. and even "cool" although I've **never** looked particularly "cool" before. At one point, I did revise my idea of cool to being a *really* competent, *really* smooth, *really* relaxed, *really* "nice" caregiver. But, this was still about me and based on pridefulness, not a healthy feeling about her needs or even what I had learned and accomplished, as I describe in "Proud Out Loud." I've gradually gotten more used to all this and accepted a goal of just doing a decent job of taking care of Susan, rather than being concerned with how I look to everyone else. I also want to put others at ease to help them relate to us more comfortably and help Susan feel as normal and a part of things as I can (she describes being disabled as like being invited to a party and then being forced to sit and watch everyone else have fun). My pride sometimes prompts me to try to look good in all this, but that's feeding another thing I say I don't want: being a "caregiver hero" as I describe in those earlier lyrics. Another pridefulness. Do you need to do a pride check, too? Boy, this all gets so convoluted doesn't it?

IT'S A SMALL WORLD

Verses:
I want to talk about my day: the clients that I've seen.
She interrupts to ask if I can see her bib's still clean.
We watch t.v.; I fill her in on what she can not see.
And right at every crucial spot, her focus turns to pee.

Chorus:
Her world is shrinking smaller, smaller, smaller as we speak.
Just as far as to her neck and how it's getting weak.
Just as far as to her feet and how they crack and creak.
Just as far as to her bladder: how it's sprung a leak.

Verses:
I try to share a song I'm writing: what the themes explain.
But her attention jumps onto her latest ache or pain.
I ask her out and make some plans for us to have some fun.
While she goes on and on 'bout what her sitters haven't done.

Chorus:
Her world is shrinking smaller, smaller, smaller, smaller still.
Down to the distance to her stomach from her mind and will.
Down to the distance to her hands that make her drop and spill.
Down to the distance to her legs that make all walks uphill.

Verses:
I invite her to a gig my band is going to do.
She'll only go if there's a restroom I can take her to.
We watch a movie on TV that's full of thrills and chills.
She mostly cares if it's too late for her to take her pills.

Chorus:
Her world's collapsing inward like a dying star in space.
That forms into a black hole 'cause the fusion can't keep pace;
That sucks in all the energy near by it in that place;
That threatens to devour her world, and mine, without a trace.
My dying star's diminishing and I feel lost in space.

I understand that Susan's profound disabilities and large collection of disorders and dysfunctions tend to make her world shrink down to all the little things that concern her well-being and comfort moment to moment. We're all familiar with, and even joke about, this same dynamic in very elderly people who seem to want to spend our visits with them discussing their latest aches and pains. All these little things like needing a potty break, wanting some water or a yogurt snack, being aware of her neck or foot hurting, wanting the TV volume turned down or the shade drawn a bit lower or noticing another bruise or needing a tissue may seem trivial; but, they are what constitute the world she lives in and can perceive and they make a huge difference in her quality of life, pitiful as it now is. And some of her lack of attention or forgetting what I'm talking about or interrupting me when I'm doing dishes or sending an email is directly related to her brain damage from the strokes.

These ought to just be minor inconveniences for me, but they also affect me emotionally. It hurts my feelings she seems to be dismissing or ignoring or losing interest in what I'm saying. Or, I get annoyed she seems so "insensitive" to my needs and agenda in interrupting me or making me stop doing dishes or laundry or playing my banjo to be able to hear her weakly speaking about another little need in her world. I react as if she doesn't care about me, when the truth is probably that she is simply dealing with what is most immediate to her; she's legally blind; and she's almost totally dependent on me for making that world as decent as possible. She can't help it that her world has shrunk so much; but, I can't help feeling left out of her world which often doesn't seem to extend to me. Is the world you and your loved one have been inhabiting together slowly shrinking? I'm afraid it's a normal thing and it goes with the territory. But, don't get down on yourself if you feel hurt or scared or sad about it.

EYES ON DEMISE

Verses:
Is it wrong to wish that someday she might wake up dead?
That all her mini-strokes might some way sum up in her head?
What if all her pressured blood got spiked 'cause she got torqued?
Systolic went all hyperbolic, bottle got uncorked?

Chorus:
*After all, it's not just what **I** sometimes fantasize,*
***She** wants it bad for both of us: her "ultimate demise."*

Verses:
What if while we're driving, some big semi I don't see,
Smacks us on the shotgun side, the sole survivor's me?
What if some tornado funnels us up in the sky,
She's stuck in Oz while I descend, quite gently, from on high?

Chorus:
*It sounds so wrong and yet I guess, **I** really realize,*
***She** truly would be happy with her "ultimate demise."*

Verses:
What if slumbering at night her apnea got deep?
Her snoring stopped and then she dropped into eternal sleep?
What if some mean home intruder carrying a gun,
Shoots her 'cause he can't include her in his plans to run?

Chorus:
***I** feel so guilty, wishing that some day she up and dies,*
*And yet, **she'd** welcome eagerly her "ultimate demise."*

Of course, I don't really want her *dead.* What I want is for her to be the way she was before she became so disabled. But, I'd also like to have the strength of my 20's, be six feet tall, be consistently kind and wise and be able to play mandolin like Chris Thile. It doesn't look like any of these are very likely any time soon. So, I guess it's natural I wish we were both out of these tough times and death seems to be the most probable way. Susan actually encourages these thoughts as she often asks me to kill her and is peeved that I'm not willing to commit murder and spend the rest of my days in prison just to oblige her with an early release. She speculates about whether a tornado could blow the massive oak tree next door down on us and take her out, but leave me. She wonders how much Coumadin or "rat poison" she'd have to take to depart this world. She speculates about whether she could just stop eating and starve to death. And, she means it. She's even got my next wife all picked out, although she has not secured the permission of that lady's husband. It's very hard for her to not be able to do anything for herself or anyone else and seeing me have to do so much for her at the cost of my own quality of life and lots of distress. So, she'd like to die. She prays for God to take her out.

On the other hand, she sure is ready to eat when suppertime comes around; she bugs me until I take her down to get her medication blood levels assessed; she won't eat two eggs because she worries about cholesterol; and she always reminds me to lock the door so a burglar won't come in and get her. Maybe it's like the old bluegrass gospel song: "Everybody Wants to Go to Heaven, But Nobody Wants to Die." Or, as Woody Allen said, "I'm not afraid to die; I just don't want to be there when it happens."

At any rate, I don't feel too bad about my occasional fantasy of her slipping into the far beyond to encounter her "ultimate demise" (that term came from a college buddy who said his "ultimate demise is at hand" each big exam as studying interfered with his partying). We both know we're just talking fantasy and we've got to get on with the business of the day.

It feels a little morbid and socially inappropriate but it's mostly just talk and I think you're pretty normal if you sometimes wish your caregivee would just sort of...die. You don't have to feel guilty about it.

WHO'S DISABLED HERE?

Verses:
My wife can do 'most nothing on her own:
Her brain has major damage from a stroke.
She needs a sitter: can't be left alone.
And so, it seems, that I'm the lucky bloke.

She doesn't have much balance when she's standing,
Her left hand doesn't work too much at all,
Her legs won't always go where she's demanding,
I'm constantly afraid that she will fall.

Chorus:
I know some brain cells just don't fire, while others aren't consistent,
She isn't being lazy or resistant.
But I still think that if I yell, she'll somehow be enabled,
Yet, **she's** the one that's 'sposed to be disabled!

Verses:
Certain things she often won't recall,
Or reinvents some history I know.
Repeating doesn't help her mind at all,
And shouting is the place I sometimes go.

It often seems her brain is out to get her:
When she's upset, she simply shuts right down.
But I keep fussing, hoping she'll do better:
I scold and play the fool and act the clown.

Chorus:
I know her hippocampus has some neurons that don't work,
She isn't being stubborn or a jerk
But I'm still mad for facts forgotten, memories she's fabled,
Yet, **she's** the one that's 'sposed to be disabled!

One of the coaches at my grandson Fritz's flag football game the other morning was constantly and loudly criticizing the kids for every little mistake they made. His assessment was correct but it was so negative. And, it had a negative effect: the kids seemed to just get real nervous and focused on not doing that one thing wrong again and risk getting publicly chastised. Some froze up altogether. It spoiled a lot of the fun, which is why I thought we were there in the first place. He did not seem to realize he could help them much more by a positive recognition of their efforts and what they were doing well and motivate them more by telling them how they could do even better next time or what would be a better action and how to do it. They were just six and seven year olds who wanted to please and learn and do well and have a good time.

It seems so wrong for me to get angry at someone for not doing something they can't do or doing something they can't control; but, I do. It seems pretty crazy to yell at someone and think that will change her dysfunction; but, I do. I'm the one who's disabled, in my thinking and reactions. I'm the one who needs more acceptance of the reality of the life we now share. And, unfortunately, my response often serves only to make things worse as it tends to make Susan more anxious. She wants to please and cooperate and not hurt me and even help me as much as she can. So, she tends to freeze up and become even more disabled in that moment. Or, she anticipates doing wrong the next time we encounter that task or function, gets anxious, and does things that further undermine her ability or just irritate me in themselves. For example, my aggravation at her speech for being so mumbled, for not giving me time to switch my attention from something else, for being too soft or halting or slurred for me to hear, makes her anxious. Then she gets indirect or afraid to ask or she waits too long, which aggravates me again. She may ask if I'm about to fool with my computer or if the potty is in this room, when she really ought to say she needs something to eat or needs to go to the bathroom. And she often misinterprets my raised voice as being mad, when I am more scared she's about to fall, desperate for her to change something she is doing so we'll avert a mess or other disaster, hurting my bad back, or just getting louder as I'm perceiving her as not hearing me.

In graduate school we looked at research that showed that, while low levels of anxiety may enhance some types of behaviors (e.g. athletics, musical performances), high levels tend to interfere with almost everything, including cognitive behaviors like remembering or problem-solving. It's a lesson I thought I learned with Susan 35 years ago when I was trying to get her to shift our manual transmission cars more smoothly and at the proper speeds. I was afraid she was going to ruin clutches over and over. So, I fussed at her over and over. Of course, that only made her anxious and try too hard to do it right and please me. That made our driving together most unpleasant and her shifting even worse. I had to accept that I was in the wrong and that the cost of my griping on her and our relationship was worse than occasionally replacing a clutch or two (which never happened, by the way). It was also disrespectful (she was an adult and not asking for criticism about her driving) and not very loving. But now, I'm having to re-learn this in the newer context of her disability and my caregiving. And, I keep goofing over and over, sometimes related to my anxiety. Yet, she's the one who's supposed to be disabled.

BALK TALK

Verse:
Sometimes she will state opinions I can not endure:
Illogical, irrational, but said like she's so sure,
Based on total lack of fact and knowledge, this I know.
Did her strokes do that much damage? Tell me it's not so.

Chorus:
There's a tone I often take; I'm sure we both can hear it.
Slightly mocking, condescending, we've both learned to fear it.
I want it to leave my mind but so far I can't clear it.
I think it's to block my feeling, so I won't come near it.

Verse:
Sometimes she'll repeat a question she should know by now,
That tells me she forgot already, though I can't see how,
Or that she isn't listening or memory banks are low.
Has her brain lost so much focus? I don't want to know.

Chorus:
There's a tenor to my voice, we both know when I use it:
Patronizing and deriding, no way to excuse it.
I wish it would go away, but I can't defuse it.
I think it's to block emotion, so I never lose it.

Verse:
Sometimes she will make a comment that will make me flinch:
That shows me she "don't get it" now; she's slipping inch by inch.
Often I'm embarrassed that her thinking seems so slow.
Will she keep on losing function? How much more will go?

Chorus:
There's an aspect of my speech she often hears as "yelling:"
Argumentative and fussing, sounds that are repelling.
I hoped it would vanish, but so far it's not dispelling.
I think it's to block sensations I find too compelling.

Verse:
Sometimes she won't step as asked to, seeming to resist:
Turns her head or bends or freezes when I then persist,
Goes the opposite direction I ask her to go.
How much more mind's yet to leave? Each day is touch-and-go.

Chorus:
There's a way I talk to her that sounds just like a creep:
So hard and harsh it almost makes you want to cry and weep.
I desire to lose it but it's something I still keep.
I think that it's to dull awareness if I go too deep.

    I've never dealt well with what I perceive as someone else's irrationality, lack of logic or overly emotional thinking, especially when they come across as totally convinced they're right, with no appreciation of how humans think, memories work, or the possibility that they are fallible and may be wrong. As you might suspect, I'm probably better at tolerating my own unreasonableness, possibly because I'm less aware of it, but I hope because I do try to examine my own thinking and accept that I can always be wrong, no matter how strongly I believe I'm right. I know that memories, including mine, can be mistaken, incorrectly stored, distorted over time or that we can actually remember something as done that was only i*magined* being done. I also know that my thinking is **heavily** influenced by emotion, just as is the case with every other homo sapiens. I try hard to think objectively, to examine the quality of my thinking and to take a tentative, scientific, somewhat skeptical perspective of my evaluations and conclusions. I also try hard to be intellectually honest, one of the most important lessons I learned from my father, who also made a concerted effort to teach me how to think well. And I think I do. I like to teach, explain and, to be honest, show off my knowledge. Oh, let's face it: I like to be right. Or maybe more correctly, it hurts me to be wrong. And, of course, I often am, even though Susan thinks I'm something of a "know- it-all" who doesn't think he's *ever* wrong. So, I greatly value the art of thinking well. But, it's a real effort on my part to handle it when someone else doesn't think the same way.

I guess that's part of my difficulty when Susan says something that strikes me as too subjective, simplistic, shallow, opinionated, judgmental, blaming, illogical, ignorant, confabulating or just plain lazy thinking. I know that her cognitive processes have been impaired through all her years of little, and not so little, strokes, including her memory, reasoning, comprehension and judgment. I also try to allow for the effects of her psychological adjustment to so much loss of function, autonomy, control and ability: she badly wants and needs to feel competent, normal and on top of something. And, I think she often asks something she already knows the answer to just as a way to manage her anxiety, stall for time, get reassurance or test out her thinking out loud. For the most part, talking with her still seems like relating to the Susan I've known and loved over 45 years and she frequently will amaze me with an insight, detailed recollection, astute analysis, perceptive question or clever zinger/joke. But, occasionally, she will repeat things or ask things or say things that really bowl me over with how off the wall, out of the weeds, forgetful or crazy they sound. For example, she's asked repeatedly if our next door neighbors are living beneath us (in the crawl space?) and has insisted our bed is slanted, higher, smaller or relocated from before (it's in the same place it's been since 1978). I make allowances for her last strokes having screwed up her sense of her position in space, her visual processing and her physical difficulty getting into bed now. But these ideas don't even make sense. Can't she see that? O.K., so why do I get unreasonably upset about this and more so with her than with other peoples' "incorrect" (to me) thinking?

I've finally come to realize that a big proportion of

this distress is probably my difficulty dealing with my own **grief** and **fear**. How much mind has she lost and how much more is yet to go? And, how will I cope with her increasingly damaged thinking and my own increasing loss of my wife and partner? How will I relate to her? How will I take care of her? How will I work out issues or problems or disagreements with her? How will I make her understand what I'm doing and why? How will I share with her? How will I come up with enough patience and understanding?

She's scaring me and I want my wife back. So, being thoroughly male, I often tend to turn unpleasant emotions of fear or sadness into the easier to deal with one: **anger**. Of course I sometimes take a little detour through sarcasm, contempt or criticism along the way. But, the big distorter of human communication is probably **anxiety**.

Rule of Thumb: if you're feeling too much anger and responding harshly, look inside yourself and see where you are too anxious or avoiding some other feeling you don't want to experience.

HORMONALLY CONFLICTED

Verse;
Her memory, libido and her left hand and left foot,
Do not work like they used to: they've somewhat gone kaput.
But the parts she needs for loving still work pretty good,
And I don't want to stop them, although perhaps I should.

Chorus:
Yes, years ago her passion and her sex drive up and left.
Her menopause and mini-strokes, rendered her bereft.
I've no desire to bedroom battle or compete in war zones.
Yet, I've got fire, I'm still a man who comes complete with hormones.

Verse:
Her loving generosity I gratefully receive.
But if she's feeling pressured, sex is something I could grieve.
I'd lovingly accept some more, of that there is no doubt.
But maybe I should lovingly just learn to live without.

Chorus:
She's pleased she helps my sex needs; as she hasn't much to share.
Yet, "sex slave" is an angry phrase she sometimes will declare.
We fuss enough, we don't need stuff about which to pick more bones,
But see, her disability does not deplete my hormones.

   This is a hard one for me to talk about: so personal and embarrassing. I guess I've never fully outgrown all the modesty and prudishness bestowed upon me in childhood by my dear but scrupulous, ultra-Catholic mother who never said the word "sex" in my years of knowing her and would probably have denied such a thing existed. But, sexuality in the context of Susan's increasing disability, has been one of the greatest sources of emotional, intellectual and ethical struggle within me, as well as tension between us, not to mention conflict in Susan's mind.

I imagine it to be a pretty big deal for many other caregivers and couples dealing with similar conditions, sex being a terribly powerful drive despite Mom's reservations. So, [gulp] here we go.

For me, the questions of what to do about our marital intimacy have triggered more guilt, anger and ambivalence than any other. What sexual drive, need and desire on her part that were not diminished by menopause seemed to have been almost eliminated by all her strokes. Being more and more dependent, and therefore under my **"control"** from her perspective, only worsened this. And, I don't think years of depression and a low quality of life helped much either. But, I still had all my desires and needs, which were only increased, if anything, by my stress and lonely responsibilities as her caregiver. When we did have intimate encounters, they were enough like old times for me and she was still able to touch me in her special way I had always treasured. She was often very pleased that she was still able to give something to me, as she had lost the capacity to do much else: chores, cooking, cleaning, etc. Physical intimacy, conversing and watching TV or grandkids together were about all that was left. She was still concerned about me and my needs and would sometimes offer the gift of intimacy, although not usually as much as I would have liked.

But, at other times, she felt very pressured by the "debt" she believed she owed me for all the caregiving services I provided for her and she felt very "controlled" and "obligated" instead of giving or sharing. When angry about this, usually in response to my anger at her "rejection" or "selfishness," she occasionally even let fly words like "sex slave" that greatly disturbed me. I wrestled with this in my own mind and conscience and we talked about it frequently, sometimes rather heatedly. I felt guilty for her feeling pressured; yet, I was quite sure her brain damage had not affected her understanding of sex and our committed relationship. I swore to myself many times that I would not show her any desire on my part, although I would continue to hope for and gratefully accept any offers she volunteered. But, as everyone knows, as time goes on a hungry or thirsty man only gets hungrier or thirstier. So, I'd get weak, or sometimes mad, and my feelings would leak out in little words or jokes or actions. "Pressures" for her.

At the time I'm writing this in 2011, I'm again resolved not to actively seek any sexual favors from her, which I am not confident I can follow through on. I've even discussed with her the option of our just agreeing our sex life is over and I think this might actually be easier than never being sure or not knowing what to expect or getting disappointed repeatedly. But, I'm afraid just one yummy meal would terminate my hunger strike, again. I could wish I didn't have the needs and desires I have, even though they are totally normal. But, I do have them; I just don't know what to do with them. I'll tell you what you can try for your sexual issues...if I ever figure this all out. Meanwhile, talk about them and, for sure, don't feel bad that you feel and want sexuality. As Susan used to say, "It's as normal as going to the drugstore for a coke." But, I never was exactly sure what that meant.

HOW DO YOU LIKE THEM APPLES?

Verse:
Fighting 'bout whose hurting worse won't lessen your distress:
I can't compare your apples with my orange juice.

Preaching that my pain's more painful makes us both depressed.
So let's declare an "apples-isn't-orange-truce."

Chorus:
Knock Knock / WHO'S THERE? / Orange / ORANGE WHO?
"Orange" you glad I've stopped preaching I hurt worse than you?

Knock Knock / WHO'S THERE? / Apple / APPLE WHO? "Apple pit" * is the place for sermons, not my home with you.

So, how do you like THEM apples... if it makes me nicer, too?

* "apple pit"="a-pul-pit": a pulpit (get it?) Hey, you try making a couple of words pun out of "apple pit."

Well, I put this in to give a different pattern to these lyrics and give you some more variety. How many memoirs or self-help or poetry or song books have "knock, knock" jokes in them? Actually it's not my favorite which is:

"Knock, knock" / WHO'S THERE? / **"Sam and Janet"** / SAM AND JANET WHO? / **"Sam and Janet evening"** (better when sung to the melody of "Some Enchanted Evening" from *South Pacific*.)

O.K., I did have a point here. When feeling sorry for myself as a caregiver, I have occasionally indulged in a little preaching or lecturing at Susan, explaining how **my** suffering in all this is worse than hers and she should feel more sorry for me. "Nobody knows the trouble I've seen" goes the old gospel song. But, it's really comparing apples and oranges. Everybody's pain hurts and it doesn't make it go away or get better knowing someone else is hurting, too, or "worse" or differently. I need to stop the exhortations, which most folks don't respond to well anyway, and do better at sympathizing with her distress and asking others to comfort me in mine. Don't you get in a competition for who's hurting the most: you're both hurting. Be good to yourself and each other.

AND ANOTHER THING

"Take care of yourself, take a break now and then,
When you take on a caregiving role."
Well, I know that's right and I try with all my might,
But, that's just another thing I can't control.

"Take care of yourself, take time for some fun,
Run a mile, take a nap, maybe two."
Well, I know it sounds good and I guess that I should,
But, that's just another thing I gotta' do.

"Take care of yourself, take a long, restful trip,
Slip away, skip and play, get a tan."
I could train someone else to handle the details,
But, that's just another thing I'd have to plan.

"Take care of yourself, take your cares to a shrink,
Think it through, don't get blue, clear the air."
She's so sad when I leave and starts in to grieve,
But that's just another thing I'd have to bear.

For me, being a caregiver means there's always something else to do. I'm a strong believer in caregivers being good caretakers of their own mental, physical, spiritual and emotional selves. I know that if I don't take care of Don, he won't be useful as a caregiver for Susan. So, as I say in "Gimmicks in Limericks," I try to do a lot for myself. I run three miles almost daily and do exercises to keep my bad back (arthritis) and middle strong and limber. I eat healthy stuff, but reward myself with an occasional treat, too (cheese curls and ice cream are at the top of the food pyramid). I have one ale a night as I'm fixing or eating supper (nature's most perfect fluids are ale, coffee and strawberry milk shakes . . .in that order). I consume some entertainment that refreshes my soul (e.g. listen to some Dave Brubeck or Alison Krauss or Brahms; watch some old Bullwinkle or Men in Black or Monty Python). I retire to my "music room" man cave and practice my mandolin or banjo or hammered dulcimer. Better still, I get together with my band mates in *Shades Mountain Air* who are almost as dear to me as my kids, grandkids and the rest of my family. I plan an activity with my local kids (David and Jennifer) or grandson (Fritz) or take Susan to Texas to see the kids and grandkids there (Paul and Christina; Jack, Mari Carmen, Berin and yet to be had grandson {since this was written, Rowan Wulf Wendorf was born in 12/13}). I write. I read things to her we both can enjoy, especially Dickens (I love to do the English accents, although it drives her nuts).

All these things restore, invigorate, stimulate, energize and refresh me. But, as you may have noticed, they all involve me doing something else, just like all my taking care of Susan does. Moreover, they all make me do more caregiving of Susan, whether planning for a sitter for her or taking care of her food or potty needs first or anticipating and dealing with her reactions to my self-care activities. It feels like there's always another thing I've *got* to do and there are a ton of things I *could* and *should* do that I've stored up over the years of caregiving, like cleaning out the storeroom, painting the house, fixing the rotted trim wood on the house, etc., etc., etc. It's like college, where you never got caught up and had everything done except for the two weeks in between semesters. So, sometimes the most helpful thing I can do to take care of myself is . . . NOTHING. Just sit and veg and think of and do . . . NOTHING. Fortunately, being male, I'm quite capable of doing exactly that and so, I do (or *don't* actually). There will **always** be another thing I've got to do. Rest, my friend. Take a break. Do some nothing. Take good care of yourself: you're worth it.

~E LIFE

~ne Eyre, AGAIN, before we hit the sack,
~e some Monty Python, even Men in Black?

Must we near MORE Willie singing, plucking "Trigger's" strings,
Or could I play some Janis Joplin? Man, how that girl sings!

Should I fix MORE fish and okra? Spicy that is not.
Or could I eat some Tex-Mex, curry, something really hot?

Will I watch TV with her, my laptop on my knee,
Or go back to my "music room," spend some time with me?

Chorus:
How much of my life, do I live for my wife, and how much for myself?
How much my own living, how much her caregiving, do I store myself on a shelf?
She's mostly got, the life I do for her; and there's lots I haven't done.
How do I live these two lives I've got to, knowing she can't live her one?

Verses:
Do I RE-READ Willie's memoir or biography,
Or could I read my Pogo comics, David gave to me?

Do I narrate one more movie, since she can not see?
Or go record my audio book I'm putting on CD?

Do we watch a Willie concert for the MILLIONTH time,
Or could I see my Brubeck video I bought online?

Do I fix her eggs and biscuits, food that's good but bland,
Or have me huevos con chorizo, wouldn't that be grand?

Chorus:

How much of my life, do I live for my wife, and how much for myself?
How much my own living, how much her caregiving, do I store myself on a shelf?
She's mostly got, the life I do for her; and there's lots I haven't done.
How do I live these two lives I've got to, knowing she can't live her one?

I have this daily debate going on in my head about how much of my time and energy I should give to Susan and how much to myself. And, how much to *us*? Not to mention our sons, their families, our siblings, their families, our neighbors, their families, our friends, their . . . well, you get the picture. At this point (around 2013), Susan can do almost nothing for herself and she cannot see very much either, all the results of her stroke damage. So, I'm excruciatingly aware that almost all of her minuscule quality of life is totally dependent on what I **do** or **don't do**. What is the right balance to hit? If I don't do enough, she has very little life and I have very much guilt. If I do too much, then my quality of life suffers even more and I have to battle with resentment I don't need to feel any more of than I already do.

Complicating this for us, is that she also has memory and attention deficits. So, right in the middle of a movie I'm narrating for her, she may ask some question about something totally different or to test her memory or try to fix facts about her age or our anniversary into her memory. And, whatever we do today, she may or may not remember next week. It's almost totally unpredictable. So, I can get frustrated that I'm doing something for her or telling or explaining something she won't recall anyway and I'll have to do it all again, maybe over and over on a semi-daily basis. Yet, I remind myself that it really does make a difference for her, all the difference really, at that **moment** it's happening. And, I do think there's a residual effect on her feelings and our relationship even if not consciously remembered. Can I be satisfied that this is enough and makes the loss of time I could have spent on myself worthwhile?

What's a poor caregiver to do? Or not **do**? What do **you** do? Should you give your loved one a life at the cost of your not having one? That doesn't seem fair or even make much sense and just how long do you think you could keep that up? I hope that you are trying to strike some reasonable kind of balance instead. And, once again, that means taking care of yourself, being kind to yourself, considering your own needs and wishes and feelings. Go for it and remind yourself you're doing a good thing for everyone involved.

MUST PLAY NOT TO WIN

Verses:
She wants me to discuss some stuff that's int'resting to me,
But loses focus in a minute, maybe two, or three.
Or maybe she'll forget it fast and later ask again.
I'm in a game which I must play but there's no way to win.

If I don't talk to her for long she feels like she's neglected,
But if I tell her what she asks, my answer is rejected.
Or maybe she'll just interrupt with what she then is thinkin'.
I'm in a game which I must play but there's no way to win.

Chorus:
I feel just like a jockey who rides horses in a race,
But's not allowed to ever win, or show, or even place,
Can never quit or rest or find another horse to ride,
And when the horse gets tired he has to run along beside.

Verses;
She daily tries to tell me just how long we have been wed,
But she's just guessing and she often gives her age instead.
She gets mad if I explain those neurons just aren't workin'.
I'm in a game which I must play but there's no way to win.

Then she tries to state her age and often gives her sister's,
But if I don't correct her then I find that I have pissed her.
And she gets mad if I then help her change the way she's thinkin'.
I'm in a game which I must play but there's no way to win.

Chorus:
I feel just like a pitcher for whom baseball is his job,
But's not allowed to throw it fast, can only toss a lob,
Can never quit or rest or find another place to play.
And has to pitch left-handed with a blind-fold in his way.

This has been an ongoing dynamic that's gotten better and worse over the years, with my reactions varying accordingly or sometimes *making* it better or worse. In so many areas I'll feel that there **is** no good response to her statements or requests or needs. Or, if there is, I sure haven't found it. Like the lyrics relate, this probably happens most frequently around all the daily litany of things she asks me to tell her or do for her or validate her memory about. She desperately wants her brain to work right and keeps trying to *make* it do so. For example, she'll say several times a day, "How old am I? Am I . . .?" and throw out a number: "66, 65, 63, 80, 86, etc." Sometimes she'll hit it or get close; but, it's mostly chance. Then she'll ask "How long have we been married" and throw out another number: "63 years" or "35 years" or "40"? She rarely gets this the first guess and generally gives a number that makes absolutely no sense, like "69" when she's just established her age as "66." I interpret that as meaning she's trying to go on just rote memory without giving it any thought to see if her guess is even reasonable. I can say, "Think a minute: how old are you? Can you have been married three years longer than you've been alive?" That's likely to make her mad. She just wants me to **tell** her the correct number and let her try to memorize it. I've learned from experience that this has never worked for her, not even for a short time, much less until tomorrow's repetition. So, I see no reason why to keep trying it. I can tell her that and suggest she come at this in a different way; but, that's likely to make her see me as oppositional and trying to give her a rough time. I can try to bow out of the whole routine, which is tempting as I can see where this is likely to go, with both of us getting aggravated at the other. That would make her feel ignored or not cared about. She "just" wants me to answer the way she wants, with her answer, not mine. At least, it feels that "controlling" to me and I already start getting irritated.

    It seems obvious to me that those particular memory neurons are not going to store and retrieve that particular information as they never have and don't now. That's just the nature of dementia. And, I know that she doesn't have the same experience of this that I do, due largely to the same memory factor. It's hard for her to grasp this fact from my saying it, which tends to make me feel untrusted and annoyed . . . again. And yet, I have to recognize that those same neurons also don't seem to grasp my explanations or suggestions in these areas and probably aren't going to, no matter how much I repeat or lecture or explain or rant or search for the right words or images or examples. I've always considered myself to be a good teacher and this is what I did as a therapist for 40 years; so, it's hard for me to let go of strengths, too. Rats! It always seems to come back to challenging **me**. I want it to all be **her** fault. So, I hate this whole routine and find it very tiring and frustrating. Don't you get tired of having to grow all the time?

We go through similar rituals and dynamics around her lack of vision (wanting me to tell her everything I'm doing), how I fix her chair (tilted back to get her neck up, which hurts her heels), how I feed her (size of the bites), what movie we'll watch, when her bath is, and so on and so on. The sad truth is that, despite all the ways Susan is still the giving, considerate, caring person I married, she is also very changed by the strokes and the years. She's much more impaired of course, but also more self-absorbed as a result: more defensive of her own turf and autonomy, more vocal in arguing or complaining in ways she never did, less flexible, less adaptable. She tries hard but she's tired and she has very limited capacity for changing. Like Norman Thayer (played by Henry Fonda) in *On Golden Pond* (a wonderful movie about aging, losing functioning and caring), she's "just trying to find her way" and doing her best and trying to hold on to who she is and what she's had. It's clear to me that **I'm** the one who has to change and **accept** that **she is how she is** and only likely to get worse. It's unreasonable for me to expect her to do or say things differently just because it's so clear to me that's likely to work better or makes more sense. And, when I can buy into that in any specific area, it does tend to smooth things out some. But, I'm also tired and limited in my adaptability and patience and I don't know how to accept that I'm married to someone who's half who I married and half someone else. I don't 'specially want to. And, I 'specially don't want to relate this to issues around our romantic relationship.

ON SHARING BODILY FLUIDS

Verses:
Sometimes Susan's bladder issues just tee tee me off.
She'll wet her chair, the bed, herself, just 'cause she has to cough,
Or sneeze or laugh or drink or think. We live in yellow mist,
I constantly am cleaning up and sometimes I get pissed.

Sometimes Susan's bowel issues make my life seem crappy:
If it's stuck or runny, funny, leaked into her nappy.
I'd like to forget it all; get fecal amnesia.
Never pour her nightcaps made of milk of magnesia.

Sometimes Susan's nasal issues make me act all snotty.
I help her blow, stop bloody flow, make it all get clotty,
Open clogs, soothe with saline, make it feel all cozy.
So how's her boogers doing now? I hate to be so nosey.

Chorus:
It's not her fault, but all the strokes; she hates it just like me.
She hates that I must manage this, be "anal" as can be.
Good thing I had two kids with dirty butts and messy sickness
Who cured me of my old aversion to the world of ickness.

First I should explain: "nappy" is the British word for "diaper" (when will they ever learn to speak English?). I used it because I needed something to rhyme with "crappy." I didn't even try to rhyme with "fluids" because it only rhymes with "Druids."

Well, this is one of the sections and issues that is "humiliating" to Susan. I guess I understand that, but this is an area of caregiving I can actually feel a little bit good about in some ways. I get tired of messing with her messes, with all the nuisance, inconvenience, interruption and work that involves. I occasionally have to remind myself that these are just the natural products of natural human processes and that I won't be contaminated, stricken with the plague or have my skin slough off because I come in a little contact with them. They're probably even good for my humility and reminding me of what's real in the universe and what my place is in it. But for the most part, I've learned, like the parent of a baby or toddler, how to just go on and do what I need to do. It's not horribly repulsive or disgusting or aversive once you start doing it and you get used to it. What may be hardest for me is that dealing with all these fluids is just very repetitive and boring. I try to handle it, like I do most things, with as much humor as possible. This ought to work well as Susan's family has always been gifted at third grade anal humor and they love to share observations, demonstrations and reflections on their own and each other's bodily processes, productions, sounds, odors . . . well, enough said. I also speak that language quite well and love "sharing" with Carol, Jeff, and Gil, not to mention our sons, David and Paul, and now with the grandkids (tradition, you know). But, Susan gets embarrassed at me talking about her personal, physiological activities, fails to see how funny it all is (imagine that) and just gets "pissed." So, I get real tired with all this. You might say I'm "pooped." Sorry.

Dealing with yucky bodily goop and goo is an area where I believe you just get muddled if you try to over-think it instead of just acting. My advice to you on this comes from an old Roger Miller song: "All you gotta' do is put your mind to it. Knuckle down, buckle down, do it, do it, do it."

CHERISH OR PERISH

Verses:
I love my little grandkids: four grandboys and one grandgirl.
They fill my life with jumping joy and set my world awhirl.
So playful, trusting, loving, giving; now I understand,
Why they're in this special class of children we call "grand."

I love my supervision group, to me they're super-duper.
I never want to miss our meetings, be a party pooper.
They always see with super vision what I need to see.
They've kept me grounded many years, maintained my sanity.

Chorus:
All these special people help me take care of my wife:
By keeping me in touch with all the goodness in my life,
Keep perspective, sense of humor, feel loved as can be.
I take care to cherish them while they take care of me.

Verses:
I love my buddies in my band; they're talented and gifted.
When I pick and grin with them, I leave with spirits lifted.
They challenge and inspire and share their creativity,
But, more than that, they share their souls, less friends than family.

I love my kids, my friends, my neighbors, people from the church.
They're always ready to step in when I'm left in the lurch.
I love the sitters and the doctors and I have no doubt,
They're always there to love and care and help me work things out.

Chorus:
All these special people help me take care of my wife:
By keeping me in touch with all the goodness in my life,
Keep perspective, sense of humor, feel loved as can be.
I take care to cherish them while they take care of me.

The Beatles sang it so right: "I get by with a little help from my friends." Especially if you include kids, kids-in-law, siblings, siblings-in-law, and grandchildren (ahhhhh, grandchildren) as "friends." It's too easy to get caught up in all the trials and tribulations of caregiving and forget there's a whole "rest of my life" going on that's good and sustaining and life-giving to help with my caregiving. I'm trying hard to learn to look for the healthy and positive and nurturing and sacred in my life instead of focusing on the trials and tribulations, which pounce into my perception with no effort on my part at all. **Look for the good** and you'll probably find some, including a whole mess of folks who want to be part of your support system.

I'll again strongly advise you to request and accept the care and giving of other people as you continue your own caregiving. You're not shirking your own responsibility and you're not Superman or Superwoman. Sometimes it's hard for givers to be receivers. Susan was never great at receiving and I'm a work in progress. I've come to see that giving and receiving are both parts of the same beautiful human dance, not separate entities. A good receiver gives the giver the gift of all the good feelings that come from giving. Don't deny other loving people the blessing of being able to serve, comfort, support, help, CARE for, love and GIVE to you.

GUILTY, YOUR HONOR

Verse:
I most always feel guilty for what I don't do,
Or for doing the things that she doesn't want, too.
Or for making her do what she don't want to do,
Or pursuing the things that I want to pursue.

Chorus:
Yes, I'm guilty, Your Honor; I know I'm to blame.
I always feel guilty; it's really a shame.
I don't mean it, I'm stressed out, please let me explain.
Can't I plead innocent 'cause I'm insane?

Verse:
I most always feel guilty for how I mistreat her:
Act cold or be rude, sort of verbally beat her,
Ignore her or scold her or simply dismiss her,
Neglect and reject and infrequently kiss her.

Chorus:
Yes, I'm guilty, Your Honor: a plea I must claim.
I mean I'm not mean but I'm mean just the same.
I'm so stressed, I've regressed and my speech is profane.
Can't I plead innocent 'cause I'm insane?

    I'm quite good at guilt. I got trained by a pro: ultra-scrupulous Mom, who considered herself the world's greatest sinner. The truth was, Mom wouldn't have recognized a good, honest sin if it ran up and smacked her in the mouth. I can feel guilty for having my health, my strength, my physical and mental abilities, my full life where I can play music, play with my grandchildren, help my kids, call my friends, email our family, drive, run, write this book, etc., etc., etc. even though it's not my fault that Susan can't. I feel guilty for not doing all the things I potentially could do to give her more life, even though I know it would mean I'd have no life, I'd soon burnout and then I'd be useless for both of us. I even feel guilty for feeling sorry for myself with how much harder my life is now, as there are so many people in the world whose lives are incredibly worse, who suffer unspeakable horrors and pain and torment. I think this is all much harder for Susan than me and she has less reserves to be able to cope with it. On the other hand, knowing that doesn't change my lot and make it better; it just helps me adjust my attitude to appreciating what I do have and making the best of it all.

    Guilt has been badly maligned by my profession as something to be eliminated, avoided or even treated with psychotherapy. But, guilt is a good, normal, healthy emotion, albeit not much fun. If you did something wrong, you knew it was wrong and yet, you did it anyway, then you ought to feel guilty. That's your conscience telling you you messed up. The feeling should last long enough for you to take responsibility for what you did and how you hurt someone, to apologize and to clean up your mess and make what amends you can and learn what you need to learn to prevent your doing it again. If it keeps on bothering you after that, then there may be something wrong and you may need help forgiving yourself or dealing with some underlying shame (not feeling guilty for the wrong you did but for who you are). Unfortunately, I do have some appropriate guilt for the way I often treat Susan, especially being critical or dismissive or ignoring or scornful or verbally unkind or losing my temper. I think I'm getting better about this and I know that retiring to lower my stress has helped. I want to be kinder, more patient, more caring. But, I also know this is something I'll grapple with indefinitely. So, I'll try to see guilt as my good buddy, helping me to change and grow. But, I don't much care for it. Good thing Mom taught me to do it so well. Thanks, Mom. Oops, more sarcasm to feel guilty for.

    Problem is: I know who I want to be and I'm not him

yet. I know, realistically, it's impossible for me or any other human being to achieve perfection; but, I feel guilty that I'm not closer. Much closer.

Tip: see if you can appropriately relabel some of your guilt as "regret." For example, instead of feeling guilty I can do all those things Susan can't, relabel it as regretting that she can't do what she'd like to but not trying to see that as somehow my fault or bad if I do what I can do.

IT'S HARD TO BE THE CAREGIVEE
Verses:
She knows she'll never drive herself to all her favorite haunts,
Never eat without my help at any restaurants,
Never mop our greasy floors or wash our dirty dishes,
Never cook a tasty meal that's healthy and delicious,
Always have to ask someone for all her needs or wishes.

She knows she'll never go to stores, put groceries on the shelf,
Take a bath or even use the potty by herself,
Never walk unaided, jump or run or climb a stair,
Pull her pants up, put on makeup, even comb her hair,
Not much to look forward to, so how is she to care?

Chorus:
Sometimes she can live her motto: "Bloom where you are planted."
Other times her outlook's blotto: gloom and doom and slanted.
Sometimes dark and dismal strife is all that she can see.
Things are rough, your life is tough, when you're the caregivee.

Verses:
She knows she'll never read another word on any page,
Never will recall her wedding day or her own age.
She always must obey me, never do what I forbid,
Be often treated like she's dumb or maybe just a kid.
Every day's another day she can't do what she did.

She knows she'll never play with grandkids, teach them what she knows,
Never really get to see them, watch how each one grows,
Never have them really know her, how she used to be.
Always have to love them through their Grandpa, namely me.
It's not an awful lot to live for, how things seem to be.

Chorus:
Sometime she can be upbeat: light and bright and happy.
Other times there's just defeat: fright and blight and crappy.
Sometimes bleak and boring strife is all that she can see.
Things are bad, your life is sad, when you're the caregivee.

Days when I feel especially sorry for myself and particularly puny, pathetic and pitiful, I've found it helpful to try to imagine what life is like for Susan **every** day. She's lost the ability to do almost anything for herself; she's legally blind; she has a lot of spotty memory loss; and her reasoning and judgment are also a little affected. She's lost her privacy, her credibility, her autonomy and her ability to do things for other people, which defines who she is. She constantly feels humiliated, controlled, useless, burdensome, afraid, lonely and guilty for not being more positive and helpful to me. But, she's retained most of her awareness of all this. Her days consist of sitting in a recliner, sort of watching or listening to TV or the stereo; being cleaned and fed and dressed and toileted and taken care of by me. Talk about **boring!!** What she has to look forward to is more of the same and, quite likely, things getting even worse. Do I think I could deal with this as well as she has and bloom where she is planted? No. You might want to try to imagine what you'd experience if you were your caregivee.

SEXED, VEXED, AND PERPLEXED

Verses:
Do we, don't we; will we, won't we?
Tell me what is right and true.
Should we, could we, what would good be?
What's a starving man to do?

It's hard not to think she's slacking
"cause I'm still so hot to trot.
It's 'cause her libido's lacking.
She can't give what she ain't got.

Build a statue to dead sex life?
That's a form I dread to carve.
Wait around until my next wife?
When's a man supposed to starve?

Chorus:
Not now, she's asleep, it's early.
Not now, she's too tired, it's late.
Not now, she must eat, she's surly.
Now she can't as she just ate.
And I'll simply have to wait.

Verses:
Should this topic just be tabled,
Put off for another day?
Sex with one so stroke-disabled,
What would all the children say?

Should I let our love life sicken,
Plan for it to die away?
There's a plot I'm sure would thicken,
What would all the doctors say?

Sex is one way we linked hearts,
But it's not the same today.
It feels strange to fondle parts
I cleaned earlier today.

Chorus:
Not now, she's upset and mad.
Not now, clothing needs a change.
Not now 'cause she feels too bad.
Now she can't, it feels too strange.
And my mind it does derange.

Well, I wrote about this issue in "Hormonally Conflicted" and I'm still writing about it a year or two later, because it hasn't been resolved. Our sexual encounters continued to be sporadic but satisfying when they happened, even with her limitations and the emotional struggles surrounding physical intimacy. I agree with the guy who said "The worst sex I ever had . . . was GREAT!" I think I'm nicer when I get it; but I'm also crankier when I **expect** it and don't get it. Touching oneself doesn't feel like being touched by someone else and I don't want to start going to a "someone else" other than Susan. I don't believe in it, even though she might actually approve it (remember that she's already selected my next wife who is also very married to another dear friend of mine). However, this has gotten more difficult as she gradually becomes less and less the Susan I married as her physical, cognitive and emotional disabilities gradually become worse and worse. So, what to do? What to do? Hormones are such a powerful influence, for good or for bad. I almost wish I didn't have them....

Almost.

SMARTER MARTYR

Verses:
How am I? I'll be o.k. Don't let it worry you.
I'll find some way, 'most any day, to do all I must do.

Now don't you fret. Have no regret and thanks so much for asking.
I'm sure I'll find some peace of mind, get good at multi- tasking.

Chorus:
'Cause no one asks a martyr to a party or event.
You see one coming and you're filled with dread.
They make you feel all guilty, all your good times they'll prevent.
They're mostly fun to torture 'til they're dead.

Verses:
Am I alright? Am I uptight? It's hard for me to see.
I'm sure in time, I'll think that I'm as well as I can be.

Am I o.k.? I just can't say. I hope somehow I'll make it.
I'll be "The Man," the best I can. Perhaps I just can fake it.

Chorus:
'Cause if you want to have some laughs, you never call up martyrs,
Even if they're clever, sexy, cute.
They make you feel manipulated, guilty, just for starters.
They're mostly fun to slowly execute.

I guess I must be smarter, to not incite violence
I guess I'll just continue...to SUFFER...[sigh]...in "silence."

    I grew up relating to a part-time martyr: my Mom. Whenever we went out to eat she'd express her choice of where to go as, "Wherever everybody else wants to go is fine with me." I'm sure she thought she was being nice to let us have our preferences and, in one sense, it probably didn't matter as she was going to read only the right side of the menu and order the absolute cheapest thing she could find. Usually that was some crummy chicken dish none of the rest of us would touch. She liked to give to, but she also liked to suffer for others a bit I think, maybe in some religious way. The rest of the family would then feel guilty and like we'd been "had" somehow or maybe had our own selfishness exposed. We'd try everything we could to get her to say her choice, like refusing to state our own until she did. She still didn't. The rest of the family would then feel kind of guilty and like we'd been duped again or had the all the responsibility for making the decision dumped on us. Eventually we'd even get a little annoyed about it and I think Mom finally got to where she was incapable of having, much less expressing, her own preferences. So, I don't think that was much fun or healthy for any of us and it sure put a damper on our partying.

I hate to admit it, but I think I got a smattering of Mom's martyr DNA. Especially when I'm feeling sorry for myself with all my caregiving burdens, I can play the martyr a bit, strictly as an amateur you understand, and try to milk others for some sympathy and babying. It does feel good to get that comforting, recognition or respect, empathy and extra help. Now, you might react with, "You're just feeling sorry for yourself." I don't know where that old saying got started. I used to tell my therapy clients that there is absolutely nothing wrong with feeling sorry for yourself; in fact, it's healthy as a self- validation. If another person was struggling with what you're suffering with, wouldn't you, *shouldn't* you, feel compassion for them? Well, you're just a person, too. It's healthy to feel compassion for yourself and affirming that you have a self worthy of compassion. The problem comes in when the other's reaction is elicited or extracted, instead of requested. Playing the martyr eases over into that territory. And, you can't use it to try to control the rest of the world. But, sometimes it's better than nothing and, by golly, I *do* deserve it.

SWEARGIVING: THE SHAME GAME

Verses:
I've fussed...I've cussed...I've pleaded and cajoled.
I lecture, conjecture, negotiate and scold.
I've shouted...I've pouted...used language crude and coarse.
I yell and compel and I holler 'til I'm hoarse.

I've moaned...I've groaned...I've bellowed and I've screamed.
I reach the kind of decibels I never would have dreamed.
I've griped...I've sniped...I've chided and rebuked.
I've lectured on and on, well, until I nearly puked.

Chorus:
Once I even pitched a fit and bellowed doom and gloom
And threw a tantrum and some pillows all around the room.
I've become a grouchy bum: too prone to spew and fume.
I've begun to be as fun as any grave or tomb.

Verses:
I've preached...I've screeched...done bawling, squalling, squawking.
I've nagged and ragged 'til I can't stand to hear my own voice talking.
Abused...accused...got ugly, mean and rude.
I've yelled and shouted 'til I felt my eyes and tongue extrude.
I've grumbled...I've mumbled...done chastening and roaring.
Verbally denounced and pounced: my God, I've grown so boring!

Chorus:
I'd like to think I'm justified by all the work that came.
I'd like to think I'm really mellow: nice and kind and tame.
I'd like to think that I'm not bad: the stress is all to blame.
But I know I've lost it and I've put myself to shame.

    I don't have a problem with the fact that I *feel* so much irritability, aggravation, hostility and outright anger.

To me, that doesn't require justification because I think anyone going through what I have been going through would feel some of those same emotions. I'd be willing to bet that you have had some of the very same feelings. I do, however, have an enormous problem with how I have *acted* in reaction. I hate it; I don't believe in it; I'm **ashamed** of it; it scares me; it makes me **furious**; and I really want not to repeat it. Most people would be amazed if they heard some of the ways I've talked to Susan and I don't think of myself as an essentially angry person. I understood Mom to tell me once in my childhood that I had an "anger problem;" but, she told me as an adult that she never said or even thought that (Sis insists that I never had any "anger problem" she can recall). I remember losing my temper a number of times with my sons when they were teenagers and doing some shouting and screaming and cussing in our arguments, especially when I was being yelled at, too. I got close to slugging one once but scared myself into awareness when I heard my brain telling my mind that hitting him was really a good idea and might just be the "breakthrough" we needed. It sure showed me my capacity for self-deception under stress. I have usually tried hard, probably even too hard (turning a difficulty into a problem), to *suppress* my anger most of my life and I'm usually seen as being unusually good-natured and even-tempered. I can flare at times, but the rare leak through when I zap someone with a hurtful zinger astounds the victim as so uncharacteristic of me. I highly value being a kind person and am generally fairly successful at that. So, I'd love to have some justification for acting so jerky with Susan.

    I am still usually able to control my mean anger at her in front of other people. They may hear some tone, but not the volume, critical scolding and harshness she gets to hear. So, why can't, or don't, I exert similar control alone with Susan at home? I've been able not to call her names, which I've always found particularly offensive, but not block all the occasional yelling and cussing and berating. Some of this is undoubtedly because I want to protect my public image; but, it's occurred to me that I may be undermining my own control by how I'm drawing the lines about what's o.k. for anger expression and what is not. I heard early on in caregiving that losing patience, getting mad and even losing your temper is a part of normal reacting to all the stress. You have to learn to accept that, forgive yourself and try harder to find ways to get some relief and not burn out. I believe all that, have given that advice to other caregivers and now give that advice to you. However, I may have to realize that I can also use that as an excuse or justification and may have sometimes allowed myself *too much* leeway in how I expressed the emotions. This issue is really distressing me at this point in our caregiving journey and I badly want to improve. There just can't be any justification for dumping my stress on her even if it feels like she's sometimes dumping hers on me (her doing something wrong doesn't make it right for me to also do wrong).

But, my supervision group also helped me see some possible errors in my thinking that I still had a reserve of self-control I was tapping into when another person was present. They suggested that the extra control was in the presence of the third person, not in me. They also encouraged me to look into whether this was a normal, albeit very undesirable response to chronic, enormous stress or if it might be that the caregiving was triggering old personal issues particular to me. I mentioned the flaring, parenting exploding and hearing as a kid about "anger" problems and I also recalled an incident around middle school when I was berated and humiliated by a bullying peer patrol-boy at a school crossing. I was so mad at his unfair, embarrassing, unreasonable, mean treatment of me I was helpless to end, that I began to cry, which humiliated and shamed me even more. I haven't gone into great depth about that but it feels like the same kind of feeling I often experience with Susan and my anger at her in caregiving. I say all this to suggest to you that you look for where you may be having your situation trigger especially troublesome reactions unique to you. This is the kind of thing you may even want to explore with a therapist. It's also quite "normal" to have a personal legacy and personal issues; but, it may need some particular attention.

I'll pass on another tip for you that helps me some. I try to monitor how *fast* I am flaring and how easy or hard it is for me to stay within my acceptable anger boundaries and cool myself down. Am I overreacting again? Can I see that it's a request for a need, not a demand, as she's helpless? Can I see that her asking for something or telling me something is reasonable from her point of view or that I'm just getting annoyed because it's interrupting my doing something I'm engaged in? Am I expecting too much of her and not accepting her disabilities or too much of myself and not accepting my own limitations? Am I overdoing somewhere or not asking for the help I need or overdue for a break?

I wrote the above several months ago. Last night I lost it the worst I ever have and said almost all the bottom line things I swore I NEVER would, even though I've been able to hold them back all these many years now. I was amazed my patience reserves were so depleted that I went so easily and swiftly into total moronic jerk meltdown. So, I guess I need to look at this the way I just suggested you do and see what I missed, what I need to examine more deeply, calm my anxiety, run this by a trusted support person, revise my expectations of her and myself, forgive myself if I can, reset my line (even though I'm scared that having crossed it once will make it too easy to cross it again) and try to move on using as much self-control as I can make myself use or develop or share with someone else. **I think the key is taking better care of myself all along so I'm less likely to ever get to this level of stress and do it whether I feel the need for it or not at the moment.** I can't be like the frog in the frying pan.

THE KINDNESS OF FRIENDS WE DON'T KNOW

Verses:
The airlines pre-board us and nicely escort us, they roll us right onto the plane.
They save us the first row and right from the get go, they save my poor back from more strain.
She goes through security, more opportunity, for our new friends to be kind.
Attendants attend her, they rush to befriend her, more niceness you never will find.

Chorus:
I greatly respect what I've come to expect:
We'll be helped out wherever we go.
I must testify on this help I rely on:
The kindness of friends we don't know.

Verses:
Little old ladies and mothers with babies, rush to hold open the door.
Men offer to lift her, each gesture a gift her neediness brings to the fore.
Cars wait 'til we're past and always unasked; the help just goes on, never ends.
Kids let us go first and our hearts nearly burst with the kindness of all our new friends.

Chorus:
I greatly respect what I've come to expect:
We'll be helped out wherever we go.
I must testify on this help I rely on:
The kindness of friends we don't know.

    Susan has always treated the rest of the world like they were her friends. It didn't matter she hadn't even met them yet and didn't even know their names: she'd know something about whomever she came in contact with by the time she left. We always joked that she was incapable of going to the grocery store without coming home with a story about some new friend she'd met. She'd know their name, their birthday, where they went to church and how many kids they had and probably about some issue or problem they were struggling with and she could help them with. I've always been more shy around strangers and preferred to do "man shopping:" go into the store to the shelf I wanted; get the item I needed; go quietly through checkout and get in my car. After 45 years of knowing Susan, I don't do that any more. It doesn't feel right to go out in public now and not strike up at least three or four conversations with the people I encounter. Now I enjoy it. Thank you, Suze.

Whenever we go out, Susan's in a wheelchair, with her head all bent over and usually with a blanket around her, even in summer. She's obviously disabled and looks like what she used to call a "character." She's legally blind, but she still tries to talk to people. Sometimes she's inappropriate in that or can't tell how they are reacting and it embarrasses me a bit. Of course, she usually gets her same old response and is still pretty much focused on them and how they're doing and if they need anything, not herself. But, we're both continually touched by how kind strangers are and how they reach out to us to offer help or reassurance or compassionate words. I'm very skilled at maneuvering her wheelchair in and out of doors or elevators or transferring her to chairs and I usually don't need much assistance. But, I know it's our blessing back to people to let them help us anyway. And, it feels good to have that caring extended to us. At this point, I have come to *expect* it and *assume* someone will offer to help and I would now be surprised if we didn't consistently experience the kindness of strangers: our friends we just don't happen to know yet. Expect people to be kind to you, too, and cherish it when it happens because I guarantee it will.

UNDULY MULEY?

Verses:
When we stand you start to bend, I always say "Stand straight."
It rarely helps but I keep fussing,
Though you get irate.

I repeat the same old warnings, give my same old fears.
I go on and on and on,
I'm talking to deaf ears.

I launch into a lecture though it often starts a brawl.
The problem is I'm scared to death
That you are gonna' fall.

Chorus:
You claim I'm stubborn as a mule,
I just won't budge; I act the fool.
My aim is not at hard and cruel,
My mind is sludge; I've lost my cool.

Verses:
I know you hate my scolding, so why do I persist?
Because it's often highly crucial,
That's why I insist.

I guess I hope that if I holler I'll get through to you.
You'll remember when it matters,
Though that's rarely true.

So I go on and give you yet again another fussing,
I badly want to have an impact,
And it beats me cussing.

Chorus:
You say that I'm a "jackass," too,
Too insistent, fume and spew.
But, hey, I don't know "jack," as you
Get too resistant, what's to do?

Verses:

When I'm helping stand you up you often ask of me,
"Put both my feet down on the floor?"
That's silly as can be.

I respond with crude attempts to tell a joke or two,
Like "No, let's hop or levitate,"
That sounds "smart-assed" to you.

I know that mostly will not work, so why try levity?
Why don't I give up being funny?
Pure anxiety.

Chorus:
You call me just a "know-it-all,"
Who acts so smart it starts a brawl.
Caregiving I don't know at all,
No steering chart, my brain's too small.
I feel my back's against the wall:
A three year old lost at the mall.
*I wish I **were** a know it all.*

Susan and I both see each other as the "stubborn" one. In my more asinine moments, (get it: ass-inine), I want to attribute it to her Scottish ancestry and being so "controlling." She wants to blame my German ancestry and "Wendorfness." Upon more open-minded, sensitive reflection, I realize that she's just trying to hold onto what she's losing or trying her best to cope with what she's lost. Or, sometimes she's just wanting reassurance about what I'm asking of her or what she's asking of herself or maybe she's just telling herself out loud what someone else might say internally. I, on the other hand, am doing my best to take care of her, accomplish the task at hand, give her some kind of quality of life and prevent her being hurt. I'm trying to stick with what hard experience has taught me works best or is safest and to make things as predictable as possible given her memory issues. I'm struggling with the daily, tedious boredom of obnoxious jobs and the endless repetition of the same comments or questions she asks over and over, as she forgets, and will forget this time, too. Or, I'm also just trying to deal with what we've lost, or I'm afraid we'll lose, by tapping into my usual coping mechanism of humor.

For example, when I ask her to stand up, she'll say "Now?" or "Straight up?" Occasionally, I'll say, "No, **yesterday**" and "No, let's **spiral** up this time." Sometimes she laughs but I can see why she sometimes sees it as sarcastic, "smart-assed" and a put down. I have to be honest that sometimes I guess it is. I really do want to lighten things and use humor to gain perspective and soften our predicament. And anxiety is still the big distorter of communication. *When you're anxious, humor can come out sounding sarcastic and biting.* But, I know there's a deeper level to all this, too. **I'm scared**. I've never taken care of anyone at this level. Pop was never quite as dependent with his Parkinson's and he handled being helped beautifully. Mom never required as much physical assistance but her Alzheimer's eventually meant she didn't have any idea what was being done or who was doing it. Besides, they were both in assisted living settings (dementia care eventually for Mom). Even taking care of our sons as babies wasn't quite like this and they were totally helpless. But, they couldn't talk and reason and have an awareness of how well or poorly I was doing. I wasn't trying to continue a marriage relationship with them, either. As I've lamented elsewhere, you don't get handed a road map or navigation chart or owner's manual when you get the medical diagnoses for your brain damage. I'm making this up as I go along and half of the time, I don't have the foggiest notion what I'm doing. The rest of the time I'm afraid of what may happen in the future and what I'll be called on to do then or what tough decisions I'll have to make.

So, I'm not really a "jackass." Well, maybe a little

"muley," but not unduly so. I'd like to think of my stubbornness as "perseverance."

Good luck, Me.

GRAVITY IS AFTER ME

Verses:
The hair that grew atop my head now sprouts from nose and ears.
I've ears like Dumbo, nose that's jumbo, rosy eyes with tears.

Places creaking, others leaking, neck has got a crick.
What if my old pancreas decides to go get sick?

I daily gain a new place pain plus ones already hurting.
What if my old back should crack, a fate with which I'm flirting?

Chorus:
Bad enough I have to caregive all her aging ills:
Bathe her, feed her, dress her, change her, manage all her pills.
*But I also have to cope with changes **I** go through.*
It's for real, I have to deal with my own aging, too.

Verses:
Focus strays, beard grays, eyebrows grow too thick.
What if my old heart or brain decides to go get sick?

Bowels slowing, lungs blowing, toenails start decaying.
Pace is slacking, memory lacking, Uhh. What was I saying?

Cheeks more blushy, muscles mushy, strength ebbs day by day.
Vision's bleaker, hearing weaker, Huh? What did you say?

Chorus:
Bad enough I have to caregive all her aging ills:
Bathe her, feed her, dress her, change her, manage all her pills.
*But I also have to plan for changes **I** go through.*
*Yes, you see, that gravity is working on **me**, too.*
And, my dear, I have fear, I can't take care of you.

As Susan's caregiver, I am acutely aware of all her medical issues, physical and cognitive limitations, daily needs of body and mind, and all the little and big things that go into keeping her going and giving her some quality of life. There are tons of things to remember, think about and plan for every day. But, I also have to look ahead and anticipate where these problems are likely to change or worsen or how she may develop new ones as the conditions evolve (or *devolve* maybe) as well as how the aging process might affect them and her. But, on top of all that, I'm also becoming more intensely aware that I, too, am aging and changing and gradually losing strength and functioning. And one of these days, I won't be able to muscle her around like I do now. I have a little arthritis in my back but am overall pretty healthy as were both of my parents well into their 80's. But, one big fall or disease could change all that. Mom had nothing much wrong with her up until her death . . . except Alzheimer's. What if I get her Alzheimer's? Who'll take care of Susan? Hey, who'll take care of ME? I may not be 66 and young and sexy forever! I'm trying to be light about this, but it's scary. Are you planning for your own aging, too?

VILE DENIAL

Verses:
I knew my words were often hateful, sometimes even vile.
I didn't know the reasons why 'cause I was in denial.

I didn't realize my anger covered up my grieving,
For all the losses in my life: my wife who's slowly leaving.

I wish I'd been aware of this and maybe then not blow it,
But you can't know what you don't know, until at last you know it.

Chorus:
A frog will stay put in a pan with slowly rising heat.
He doesn't know his goose is cooked until you've fried his feet.
A cozy cage is hard to vacate, 'least not for awhile.
You don't get out 'cause you don't know you're stuck in deep denial.

Verses:
I saw how I was acting mean, not usually my style.
I didn't see the reasons why 'cause I was in denial.

I wasn't clear my ugliness had camouflaged my grief,
For losing my dear wife to to strife from her disabling thief.

I wish I'd had more insight here and maybe then not flee it,
But you can't see what you don't see, until at last you see it.

Chorus:
A closed-up idling car's exhaust can slowly hurt your head.
You don't know you're in fatal slumber 'til you wake up dead.
A snuggy snare is tough to leave, it doesn't vex or rile.
You don't get out until you see you're stuck in deep denial.

I've been submerged in Egypt's River, like a crocodile,
Never knowing I was swimming, deeply in de Nile . . . until I emerged . .

I've written of my struggles with my irritation, outbursts, even tantrums, rants and raves and rages. I've felt very guilty and embarrassed about them. I blamed them on my lifelong short fuse that occasionally gets lighted and all the stress, anxiety, responsibility, frustration, etc., etc. in caregiving that stretches my patience and courage. I've become increasingly aware that much of my anger has been the surface layer over a lot of anxiety about some disaster about to happen in the moment (e.g. a fall) and what is likely to happen in the future (i.e. she'll get a whole lot worse). It's probably more denial about how terribly hard this all really is, for both of us, despite my trying to keep a positive and optimistic attitude and think I can handle this just fine ('cause I'm so big and tough and strong and healthy) and other people have it much worse anyway. But, I'm realizing the anger has also probably been a coverup for the sadness and realization of loss that was much harder to deal with. In other words, I've been **in denial** about being **in mourning.** As the tired joke goes, like Cleopatra, I'm the Queen of Denial. I haven't really wanted to handle the fact that I'm slowly losing the wife, friend, companion I've been married to so many years and that I'm losing some of my own choices, independence and opportunities along with her. So, I've then unfairly berated myself for my denial. After all, I'm a "shrink:" insight is my business. But, I can't expect myself to have insight until I see what I haven't been seeing, until it's all *in sight:* out of denial.

You can't know what you don't know before you know it. The knowledge may have been there all along, but the essence of denial is not letting yourself in on your own secrets, at least until you're *ready* to accept them and deal with them. You don't choose denial; you become aware you've been in it when you start to come out of it.

Rats, I guess I'm ready. Now, don't you get down on

yourself if you realize you've been in denial. Just move on with what you now know, even if that means you need to grieve, too.

SERIAL GRIEVING

Verses:
Dead folks ain't supposed to ask to have their diapers changed.
They're not supposed to aggravate you 'til you feel deranged.
They should be silent as the grave, never make a sound.
Corpses are supposed to stay there: six feet underground.

Dead folks ain't supposed to ask to have you wipe their nose.
They're not supposed to agitate you, messing up their clothes.
They should be silent as a cave, never make you toil.
Corpses are supposed to stay there: six feet in the soil.

Chorus:
Grieving warps when any corpse, just won't stay beneath the ground,
Who's popping up and hopping up and always flopping 'round.
Who meets and greets, is quite alert and won't accept a dirty bed.
How to grieve and be bereaved, when corpses won't act dead?

Verses:
Deceased bodies ain't supposed to lose more body parts.
They're not supposed to keep on while each arm and limb departs.
They're not expected to partake in merriment and mirth.
Corpses are supposed to stay there: six feet in the earth.

Deceased bodies ain't supposed to keep on needing tending.
They're not expected to need feeding, medicine or mending.
They should be easy, never take a bath or sweat or hurt.
The dear departed are supposed to stay six feet in dirt.

Chorus:
Caregiving someone living, is a constant grieving thing:
More creaks and squeaks, more trips and slips, more losing zip and zing.
More pain/ less sane, as all they are just slowly fails and falls away
How to grieve and be bereaved, they bite the dust each day.

How to grieve and be bereaved, not hope and wish and not pretend,
*When here today, half gone tomorrow **mini-deaths** don't end.*

    Whoa, where did all that come from? I chose the dark humor because the grieving process I brought up in the last lyrics is so hard and painful to deal with straight on. I used to tell my clients that divorce was a lot like a death: the death of a marriage with all its plans and dreams and future. I said they had to grieve, just like with a death. But it sure was a lot tougher to do when you have kids and the corpse, your "ex." keeps showing up every other weekend for visitation. With usual bereavement, you go through horrible sorrow but it very gradually gets better and you're eventually able to move on in your life. Even harder are situations like a soldier missing in action or a family member who runs off or is abducted and never heard from again. There's no closure, no end point and the grieving goes on and on.

    Caregiving can be something like that when the person you love is gradually losing a little bit of ability and life each day and you're gradually losing little pieces of your relationship along with it: "a quarter of an inch at a time." Just as you get one loss mostly grieved and adjusted to, another chunk dies. But, this process goes on and on with no real closure and no real end point. So, to some extent, you stay in grief mode continuously while you're still trying to have a relationship with the person and what functioning is still alive. Susan's mother used to play a game with our boys where she'd take the last piece of cake or brownie, cut it in half and eat the half. Paul would cut that piece in half and eat it. David would cut that piece; Mama would cut that one and so on. They'd get down to protons and electrons; but, eventually one of the three would laugh and just grab their morsel and eat it, which ended the game. This caregiving feels like that except we NEVER get down to the last bite. We're down to the quantum level but there's no real end in sight: no closure, no real moving on. Sometimes, "t'ain't easy" and if your situation is like this progressive losing and grieving I'm dealing with (or trying to), I'm afraid you need to let yourself feel sad; search out what is still alive to connect with in your caregivee; and let others comfort you. But, accept your grieving.

SAVE 'EM FOR THE END

Verses:
A lot of folks will offer to come help and baby sit her,
Saying I need breaks or I'll get cranky, maybe bitter.

They see me as never letting others do enough.
I think I'm o.k. for now 'til things start getting tough.

I'm afraid I'll wear them out or lose them as a friend,
So I figure I should wait and save 'em for the end.

Chorus:
What if something happened to her, somehow she got hurt?
Someone gave her too much thinner, made her blood all spurt?
Sometime dropped her, broke her arm, her leg or hip or head?
Fell asleep and didn't notice she was turning dead?
Who didn't take good care of Susan 'cause they knew not how?
You think I should let them come and get some training now?

Verses:
I know no one else can do it half as well as me,
Get each little detail right, care as carefully.

So half my epitaph will say I kept my foolish pride.
I held it tight with all my might, not knowing I had died.

Spurned assistance with resistance, did it all instead.
The other half will simply laugh at how I turned up dead.

Chorus:
What if something happened to **me**, somehow **I** got hurt?
Somehow sprung a leak and all **my** blood began to spurt?
Sometime fell and broke an arm, a leg, a hip, a head?
Fell asleep one night and then the next day woke up dead?
Who'd take care of Susan and just how would they know how?
You think I should let them come and get some practice now?

Well, I just re-read the much earlier selection, "I Can Do It All." I guess I haven't come real far because I'm still basically trying to do it all several years and several additional strokes later. I even retired to be able to do it all. And, it does still seem overwhelming to teach someone else all the hundreds of little details I have to remember to take care of Susan the best way I've learned how and the way she expects and likes and counts on. Examples: be sure the sock isn't folded under before you put the shoe on: use the smallest teaspoon and tell her what each bite is and alternate bites with a sip of liquid; have her lean way forward as you haul her out of the chair and not stiffen or push with her one good hand until you tell her on the way up; rotate the type of pain patch on her neck so it doesn't damage her skin; put the red pillow under her ankles but not under the shoes so they don't rub her heels; monitor her feet while walking as you may have to tell her to move the left one more, etc., etc., etc. She says I should get others to help more or even put her in a senior living center; but, I think she'd be even more lonely and miserable there than she is here (I doubt I'll find a nursing home where someone will change her Willie Nelson cd every hour, much less listen to them with her). And, she's always telling me how much she needs me and I'm pretty much the only thing she has left in life and how scared she is when I am away. I realize some of that is dependency and the predictability does relieve some of her anxiety. I know, too, I **have** to get away some and that's good for both of us and that other people can do a perfectly adequate job and she will survive my short absences just fine. Paul and Christina even offered to stay with her so I can be by myself a few days in the Smokys (they live a thousand miles away and have four kids). I do go off to walk/run or get groceries or play short band jobs and I do get others to stay for longer errands or gigs, especially David and Jennifer or Sis. But just one female isn't strong enough to lift her now and she's still embarrassed about

David taking her to the potty ("Mom, I'm a firefighter/paramedic; there's not much I haven't seen"). And, she has known me now for 45 years, so she is kinda' used to me and mostly trusts me. But, I still worry about what if something happens to me, as does Susan. If I'm not mistaken, trucks can run over caregivers just as easily as someone else. I probably ought to write out a complete set of directions and update them weekly and train two or three other caregivers with supervised experience. Right. I'll get right on that.

I've now been retired a year and I'm still wrestling with how to divvy up my time. I'm trying to see my caregiving as my #1 job; but, that doesn't require my every second being devoted to Susan's care, which would drive us both nuts. There are tons of things I want to do with my own life: get this book out; promote this and the first book; record some of the selections from both and maybe even do audio books; learn my new mandola more and enhance my playing on about a half-dozen other instruments; keep up my walking and running; enjoy my friends and kids and grandkids; hike some mountains and backpack if I still can; read a ton of stuff I didn't while I had my career and family; etc., etc., etc.

It's a constant struggle with doing what I need to, what is right and I have to, what I want to, what is good for each and both of us and not feel too resentful or guilty or selfish. I do ask for and accept some help but I don't want to overly burden anyone else the way I sometimes feel or burn them out. I don't want son David to resent son Paul that he's carrying too much of the load just because Paul moved 1000 miles away and I'm real aware that someday somebody may have to take care of me. Besides, as a parent and grandparent (and sibling to Sis and Bob), there's so much I still want to do for my family. So, I tend to "save 'em for the end." If you do that, too, then you might wonder with me if we'll really know just when that "end" gets here.

I took my own advice here and asked Sis about other people helping Susan, like her. She reassured me it is NOT a huge "imposition" to others and others don't experience taking care of her temporarily the way I do on a day-in, day-out basis. In fact, Sis said she **"treasures"** her "babysitting" (Susan's term) time with Susan when she can say or do something that makes Susan laugh or enjoy herself or tap into the "old Susan." For example, Susan will ask Sis how things are going in her life or how she "feels" about something personal: i.e. *give* to Sis in that old Susan way that means so much to her. For Sis, it's not just enjoying being altruistic and helping, it's an intimate visit with the person she thinks of as the sister she never had. According to Sis, Susan sometimes even acts differently when I'm not there: a little more functional, more self-reliant, more at ease. My absence probably takes away some of the dynamics in our relationship that can make Susan more anxious, needy and dependent. In other words, when I ask for help, EVERYONE BENEFITS: me, the other helper and Susan, too.

You see how mixed up my feelings can get? O.K., I still do believe I can take care of Susan better than anyone else and give her the best quality of life possible now, at least on an everyday, ongoing basis. And, you are probably right if you think you can do the best caregiving for your caregivee and that it would stress and stretch others to try to learn and do what you do. I think everything I said above has validity and is trying to protect my family, too. And, I WANT Susan to have the best life she can. But, you and I need to continually question whether we are hitting the right *balance* between "saving 'em" and saving ourselves, because if we don't take care of ourselves, we might not be around for whenever that "end" comes. If we burn out, we're useless and other helpers don't have to provide care exactly like we do anyway. In fact, sometimes the differences may even be advantageous. So, ask for periodic, temporary help: it's part of saving *yourself* for the end and remember what Sis helped me realize: everyone benefits. Asking for help *is* doing a good job.

LESS THAN GREAT EXPECTATIONS

Verses:
I'm less prone to lather, if I expect some blather,
I'm less apt to wither, if I expect some dither.
I don't go to sniping, if I expect her griping.
I am less irascible, if I expect irrational.

Bridge:
If I show respect, then her trust is enabled.
If I can expect, that she'll just be disabled.

Chorus:
I'll not be disappointed and will feel much less vexations,
If I can settle for much less than great expectations.
When I don't expect too much, then much more can arise:
Out will ooze some former Suze just like a sweet surprise.

Verses:
My yelling's not excessive, expecting she's obsessive.
I don't start to vex, if I don't bank on sex.

I'm less apt to vent, if I presume her back is bent.
I'm less prone to nag, if I assume her neck will sag.

Bridge:
If I show respect, then her trust is enabled.
If I can expect, that she'll just be disabled.

Chorus:
I'll save myself from more of my less than great frustrations,
If I can settle for much less than great expectations.
When I don't expect too much, then much more can arise:
Out will ooze some former Suze just like a sweet surprise.

  I've figured out that I'm much less likely to get mad or sad or act bad if I can examine my **expectations** of Susan (I've always called her "Suze" as did her father, "Saint Robert") and learn where I need to change them. Remember that I married Susan because she, in addition to being so physically attractive to me, was highly intelligent, extremely compassionate and empathetic, unusually forgiving and perceptive and sensitive and positive and giving and well-intentioned and reasonable and the most loving, caring person I'd ever met, not to mention such a fun and comfortable companion. She had her faults, of course, just like everyone else, as well as insecurities and anxieties and less than perfect communication and expressing and negotiating skills. She could even be a little judgmental or opinionated or pushy. But, overall, she was usually way ahead of me and I came to rely on her to be all the things I had valued about her in the first place.

When she first got diagnosed with Alzheimer's, my greatest fear was that some day she would no longer know me and trust me. If that happened, I couldn't see how I would be able to take care of her. As you will recall, we found out several years later she had stroke problems (related to antiphospholipid antibody syndrome), not Alzheimer's, and she did not progressively and rapidly decline as predicted. In fact, she even made some slight improvement in some areas, as you see in stroke recovery. Things were still difficult, with her seizures, mild memory loss, inability to drive for herself and all her other medical problems. But, our relationship seemed to go on without major impairment and we could still enjoy our marriage and friendship much of the time.

However, as time went on, she had more strokes and more damage to her brain and more compromised and impaired functioning. It's real complicated and confusing: she's still the Susan I've always known and she's also not the same Susan, simultaneously or alternately. One minute she may come out with an astute analysis of a current political crisis and the next she may ask me if our neighbor's house is still underneath our bed (in the crawlspace?) or if the people "below us" (in the crawlspace?) will be disturbed by her Wille Nelson CD (see how that old caring about others stays no matter what?). Today she might zing me with a snappy, clever retort and tomorrow she may ask if she should help me stand her up by putting her feet on the floor (as opposed to the ceiling?) She'll express heart-felt sorrow at her inability to do anything kind to help a friend in need; then she'll give a tacky or judgmental opinion about my behavior. The other day she insensitively told me two of the songs on my band's latest CD were "awful" although I hadn't asked for feedback and they were two I sang lead on! She'll thank me profusely, and I believe totally sincerely, for changing her diaper or feeding her or putting her clothes on: simple responsibilities of my "job" I HAVE to do daily. Then, she'll turn around and nag me about making a call for her I think is a bad idea or giving her a snack I think inadequate or seem to demand instant compliance with her desire for me to put on her lipstick or give her a breath mint. She'll be very concerned and solicitous about whether she is stepping on my feet as I muscle her to the potty but not straighten her back and neck instead of hanging on my arm, which would really make for less strain on my over-stressed back and knees (that I've had flare up very badly several times, such that sometimes I even had to stop my running that I really count on) even when I ask her to. I'll give her a direction, like "O.K., stand up" and she'll ask "Now?" Then she'll anticipate my next direction to "Sit down" about two steps before we get to the chair and try to sit on air. Imagine what **that** does to my back and knees!

    I asked her about some of this tonight, like why she says "Now?" when that is totally obvious. She was very helpful. She said, "If you'll just remember I'm not ever doing it to be bad." I pursued it a bit more and she added, "I don't ever want to do anything. I'm scared of everything." She explained that she dreads most of what she has to do or I ask her to do as it's so hard, she's so afraid she's going to do it wrong and upset or disappoint me or she's scared she might hurt me. And, she's exhausted. So, "Now?" and all the other obvious questions she already knows the answer to, is another way she tries to manage her *anxiety*.

She's not trying to be resistant or too lazy to think for herself or passive-aggressive or mean. The underlying core is still the same old Susan and I have to **expect** that as her default setting, despite the momentary evidence to the contrary.

So, who's at the *core* of your caregivee? Can you ask them **why** they're doing or not doing something that bothers you and believe their answer is the truth, at least in their eyes? For me, my lyrics "Painted Bits of Bark and Stone and Tin" encapsulate the core of who Susan is (along with the old Shaker hymn "Simple Gifts") and I find it helpful to bring that to mind when I am struggling with the current Susan. You might use some of your creativity to come up with a metaphor or symbol or song or image or something that captures for you the core of your caregivee, that made them your "loved" one in the first place. Then, try to pull that up when you're having trouble with how they're acting in the moment.

DO I LOVE HER, MORE OR LESS?

Verses:
People "ooh" and "ahhh" and say "See how much they care?"
"Aren't they so devoted" and "They're such a loving pair."
It makes me uneasy, makes my "guilt-o-meter" spike.
I don't often feel "in love" or even much "in like."

Yes, I do my best in helping meet her every need:
Clean and bathe her, dress and potty, water, walk and feed,
Listen to her, read to her and narrate the TV,
Hold the phone and tell her what's been going on with me.

Chorus:
Where did all my feelings go I always felt before?
Did they sail away to some exotic, distant shore?
Did they drown in tidal waves of daily work and chore?
Die in fright of further loss and fear of what's in store?

Of course I'll keep fulfilling all the wedding vows I swore.
But will I ever feel the feelings from our days of yore?
If you know the answer, then please tell me, I implore.
It bothers me when I can't FEEL I love her any more.

Verses:
Do I do it out of pity, duty, force of habit?
Rather than because I love her? I'm not sure, dagnabbit.
Is it just because I know that it's what really right?
Or to look good, play the hero? Man, does that sound trite.

*I still **want** her welfare, health and happiness in life.*
I still try to shield her from all stress and strain and strife.
I still hope to save her from as much pain as I can.
I'll take care of her forever, that's my vow and plan.

Chorus:
I fear I'll never feel again that she's whom I adore,
Not enjoy her company the way I did before,
Just accept I love her now in mostly doing for,
But I don't like when I can't FEEL I love her any more.

I suppose I know, intellectually, that I still love Susan. Sure, part of why I work so hard as her caregiver is because I made a commitment to her at our wedding, because I loved her, to put her needs and feelings and growth and health and desires and life agenda up there at the top of my priority list, where my own are. And, I promised to always do that and do whatever it takes to keep our relationship solid and ongoing. I believe in honoring my commitments, just as I've always trusted her to honor hers. I even had some awareness at the time that eventually one (or both) of us would get old or sick and need caregiving and I was prepared to accept that as part of the contract.

But, it's more than that. I also *WANT* for her to feel better, enjoy her life, not hurt, experience some meaningfulness, see how she still has a lot to give others in her ability to accept, support, care for and forgive. I feel BAD when she feels bad. Some of that is compassion and empathy I'd feel for anybody; but, I know her so well I know what **her** life is like now and would do whatever I could to make that different, including with considerable effort and sacrifice on my part. I do my caregiver job as well as I can, partly out of pride maybe, or sense of responsibility or guilt when I'm not, but also because I really "get" how much her life depends on what I do or don't do and exactly how I do it. I WANT to GIVE her the best life possible. So, I go extra miles when I could get by with a lot less sweat on my part. Some people say love is a verb: an action word. Well, I'm sure doing lots of action!

And does Susan still feel love and like for me? Is it just dependency and neediness and helplessness and anxiety or does she still **really** know **me** and care about **my** needs and wishes and life agenda? I get moments I experience that she does, like when she's so solicitous about my back and is she helping me enough to pick her up and do I want to share her milkshake. Other times she can seem very self-absorbed and insensitive to me and my feelings, as I write about in several other selections, above. Her life is very hard and just getting through the day tires her so much she often doesn't have a lot left to give. So, it's sure not like before. During our marriage this woman actually bought me a didgeridoo, a musical saw, and a bowed psaltery. Bigger than that, she actually spent years listening to me practice the banjo!! Man, love don't get much bigger than that! On the other hand, our whole marriage she had things she didn't like about me, just like in all relationships, and she was not always easy for me to please. She never really liked my being so loud and forceful in my anger, my getting too hyper, high and comedic in social situations or my not sharing all her beliefs and ideas about things. I never was "Saint Don" and a copy of her father, "Saint Robert" who, I gather was far more reserved, non-assertive and more comfortable letting Mama take the major lead. Reportedly, he never really expressed much anger, either. And Susan, for all her uniquely wonderful qualities, was not ever "Saint Susan" either and it's not right for me to expect her to be, especially given all her cognitive changes, depression and stressful, crummy quality of life now.

In one of my favorite musicals, *Fiddler on the Roof,* Tevye and his wife, Golde, met on their wedding day. The marriage was arranged by the matchmaker and their parents told them that they'd "learn to love" each other. Twenty-five years later, their daughters start getting married, not to matchmaker selections, but out of "love." Tevye gets to wondering and asks Golde, "Do You Love Me?" in a very touching song. She's never considered it but she begins to wonder, too: "Do I love him?" She sings that, for twenty-five years she's lived with him, worked with him, starved with him, raised kids with him, shared her bed with him: all the things a good Russian Jewish wife does. She concludes, "If that's not love, what is?" And she realizes and sings, "I suppose I do." He replies, "And I suppose I love you, too." Together they sing, "It doesn't change a thing . . . but even so . . . after twenty-five years . . . it's nice to know." And, they share that knowing.

Now I'm doing all the things a good husband and caregiver does, too, and I'll go on doing them. But, I'd like to experience more often that she and I still like and love each other. It wouldn't change a thing, but even so: after 42 years, it'd be nice to know. And to **feel**. I've felt guilty for not feeling more love and like; but, I think a fair amount of that is probably more sadness for what we had that is being slowly eroded and diminished.

FEELINGS FATIGUE

Compassion fatigue is tiring me out.
Compassion is leaving no room for no doubt.
As layers keep peeling my heart needs more healing,
Before my compassion's completely tired out.

Courage fatigue is wearing me down.
My smile once courageous is turning to frown.
I'll stop going nuts and stop goosing my guts,
Before all my courage is wholly worn down.

Patience fatigue wants to shrink me away.
It's mushing me into impatience puree.
I must stop my nerves draining all my reserves,
Before all my patience has shrunken away.

Kindness fatigue is eroding me down.
My sunny demeanor's turned arid and brown.
I must get my sweetness back up to completeness,
Before all my kindness erodes me all down.

Feelings fatigue is draining me dry.
No one's immune here, not you and not I.
I need to get rest to keep doing my best.
Before all my feelings have drained me all dry.

    As a psychotherapist I was trained to watch out for "compassion fatigue." Being compassionate, kind, understanding, patient and courageous all day with clients takes a lot of energy. It's rewarding; but, it's very tiring. And, that tiring can have a cumulative effect over years of doing therapy to the point that you can get compassion fatigue and "burnout." So, we learn how to take breaks, deal with our feelings, seek consultation when things are tough, recharge our emotional batteries, know our limitations and nurture our own emotional health. Well, the same thing is true with one person taking care of another person over time. This can happen even if it's someone you love, you are committed to your caregiving, you are physically and emotionally healthy and you are doing a good job. It still uses a lot of emotional energy and it's tiring. So, the basic advice we hear early in our caregiving remains true: you have to be good about taking care of yourself and do it on an ongoing basis. I retired as a therapist when I could (turned 65 in 2012) as I was finding it too emotionally draining trying to be a good therapist all day and a good caregiver all the rest of the time. It helped, but not quite enough, and I am still working on it. And, I'll ALWAYS have to keep on top of it. And, you probably will, too. But, YOU CAN.

A MILE IN HER MOCCASINS

Verses:
When I help her stand, from the chair or the bed,
She asks where to place both her feet, arms and head.
She asks when to bend and push up with her hand,
Although it's the same thing each time that we stand.

Sometimes I'm annoyed with her, not kind at all.

Then when she's ready to sit down again,
She drapes on my shoulder and hangs by her chin.
She starts to flex knees when we're not even there.
It makes me so mad: is she sitting on air?

So I start to rant and to make her feel small.

*But I grew aware of how **this** boy now stands:*
I'm cautious to lean and use both legs and hands.
I don't have a problem, no fall and no scare,
Yet, I fear a muscle or tendon could tear.

So, how must **she** feel always fearing a fall?

Chorus:
I told you before of my "feelings fatigue"
That helped me a bunch and I mean major league.
Now look in YOURSELF and tell someone YOUR news,
*Once **you've** walked a mile in your caregivee's shoes.*

Verses:
When I help her stand, and get ready to walk.
She'll start on her waddle, then suddenly balk.
She'll turn to the side so I won't hit her nose,
Although that's the way that her body then goes.

Sometimes I'm annoyed with her, not kind at all.

Then when she's walking she'll suddenly freeze

She leans and goes limp which plays hell with my knees.
She ceases her plodding and I take her weight.
It makes me so angry: a thing I just hate.

So I start to rant and to make her feel small.

*But, I've grown aware of just how **I** now walk:*
I'm careful and watch every step like a hawk.
I don't have impairment, it's rare that I stumble,
Yet, I'm scared I'll trip and I'll slip and I'll tumble.

So, how must **she** feel always fearing a fall?

Chorus:
I told you before of my caregiver burnout
That helped me a bunch keep on giving a durn 'bout
My caregive's feelings I hope you can use,
*To go walk a mile in **your** caregivee's shoes.*

I've been a runner since high school track in 1962. I didn't know that most people eventually stop and it's always been a very effective means of exercising and keeping myself healthy in body, soul and mind. More recently, it's been one of the few times other than work, when I can really be by myself and let my mind rest. I've even written lots of my lyrics while running. But, the past few years, I have several times had to yield to the pressure of Achilles heel tendonitis, work and caregiving schedules, and injuring my knees or back or shoulders hauling Susan around and go through periods of power walking, using an elliptical trainer or stationary bike or even goofing off. I've always gone back to running when I could and I eventually found that minimalist or barefoot running took care of the tendonitis I'd had for years. I like the running as it's efficient and I also want to be able to keep up with the grandkids as long as I can. But, as Susan has gotten more impaired, it's happened more and more that I have to go back to more walking. And, at 66, I've increasingly found that things are different for me now, too. I don't feel as secure running, or even walking, when the surface is wet, much less when it's muddy. Stretches I used to plow through without thinking, I now navigate very cautiously, even slowing to a walk or going around it, after I first stiffen and alter my whole stride. If I slip or slide even a bit I go into a geezerly startle and stumble. I'm afraid to fall, which could HURT! But, even more than that, one bad injury could mean I could no longer muscle Susan around and we'd have to get more help or even look to a facility, which I sure do not want to do as I think it'd make her life even more miserable than it already is.

This new **self-awareness** has been helpful, however, as it has given me a deeper compassion and empathy for Susan and what she has had to go through every single day for a very long time. She's **constantly** apprehensive about falling although, true to form, she may be even more afraid of hurting me than hurting herself. In *To Kill a Mockingbird,* Atticus Finch is teaching his children, Scout and Jem, to try to see things from the perspective of whomever they're trying to relate to: "First of all," he said, "if you can learn a simple trick, Scout, you'll get along a lot better with all kinds of folks. You never really understand a person until you consider things from his point of view . . . until you climb into his skin and walk around in it." That's wise advice just in general, but it's particularly relevant for figuring out how you should best relate to the spouse or parent or child you're taking care of. See where they're coming from and why they may be doing what seems reasonable or best or just what they're capable of in their eyes. In other words, walk a couple of miles in **their** moccasins. You already know what your own feel like but use that, too, to try to learn about your caregivee's.

FINALE

I'm not real sure how or when to end this book because the **story** isn't over. Things keep going on and new things happen and change and old abilities are lessened or lost. I keep having new experiences and emotions and learning from them to understand myself, Susan and our feelings better. It looks now like the story will probably go on for some time to come. I'm not real into posthumous publishing and, if this is going to be useful to anyone, I don't want to make you wait or go through a trial I might help prevent or at least ease. So, this looks like as good a place to stop as any:

And so, we lived happily ever after. The End.

Well, that's not *entirely* accurate. I wish I could leave you with a wonderful outcome where everything is just great; Susan had a miraculous cure; or I got on top of it all and figured it all out and succeeded her Dad as "Saint Don." But, we'll always be a work in progress, at least I hope we'll always progress. Maybe I'm more in denial than I've realized, but I think we're doing "o.k." with what we have to deal with, which is probably the best that could be expected for us and maybe you, too. Our situation really is quite difficult. I'm not very pleased with my temper issues (had my worst blow up ever two weeks after I wrote this) but I do feel I'm getting better and there are many, many good things going on in our lives (kids, grandkids, friends, family, my band, neighbors who visit Susan, Willie Nelson still recording more cd's, etc., etc.). It may be unrealistic, given that another stroke could easily leave her bedridden or a fall could leave me unable to muscle her. Our kids want to know what my "plan" is and I hate to tell them I don't actually have one. But, somehow, I'm not all that pessimistic (denial is a beautiful thing).

I also wish I could leave you with some brilliant

insights and wise advice; but, I've pretty much given you any of that I've got already. Just **take care of yourself**: you deserve it and your caregivee needs it. Be good to yourself, be compassionate to yourself, be kind to yourself, give yourself a break. Exercise daily; express your feelings; get some rest; do something creative; learn to play banjo and eat an occasional pie. **Remember that your feelings are tough but normal; you can handle them; and you are not alone. Ask for help.** Ask for listening and understanding; ask for sympathy and comfort. Remind yourself often that there is good to be found and that you are doing a good thing. Recall why your loved one is your "loved" one.

So, I'll just say "Goodbye" for now. Maybe a few years from now I'll see you in a followup book: *Caregiver Carols 2: The Return of the Bride of the Son of the Revenge of a Musical, Emotional Memoir--the Sequel, Prequel and Tranquil.* Meanwhile, as we say in the South:

"Bye, y'all come back now, you heah?"

POST SCRIPT

Susan died quietly in her sleep on 3/5/2014, in St. Vincent's Hospital, less than a month after I wrote the first draft of this Finale. I was there holding her hand, along with son David and our daughter-in-law Jennifer, when she just stopped breathing. The previous week or so she had had a runny nose and cough I first attributed to Spring allergies, until her breathing got more labored and she quickly got weaker. When I took her to the ER I figured she had pneumonia and maybe another little stroke. She did have pneumonia, but, I was stunned to hear that she also had sky high potassium, failing kidneys, pulmonary edema, congestive heart failure and anemia. No new stroke, but maybe the wearing down of her body from the damage and sedentary life produced by years of strokes and disability. I had no idea she was so sick. Maybe I'd have gotten less angry the previous two weeks if I had known. Maybe not, as I'd let myself get way too stressed. We had the choice of very nasty intensive treatment with a shunt and dialysis and horrible medications that would produce constant diarrhea. The best this could do, however, was to put her back to the previous month when she was praying to die. And, she still had to face the same future of getting even more disabled and miserable and ending up in a nursing home when I could no longer take care of her myself. The other choice was to not treat anything and let her go. This sounded like exactly the sort of exit she had wanted for so long and the kids and Susan and I agreed to let her have that chance when the doctors assured us they could let her die with no pain and no fear. My last caregiving decisions and efforts were in the hospital over the next few days, although I had the constant help of David and Jennifer and our dear friend Sabrina.

Susan left this life much the same way she lived it. In that sense, her "heart" never really did fail. She repeatedly asked the nurses if they were too tired and if she was being too much of a burden. She apologized to everyone who visited for causing so much trouble. She could barely talk but she also managed to advise one friend to spend more time with her mother and another to be nice to his wife and she told me once to stop talking about her (she had always hated being the center of attention) and to stop being funny. So many people came to see her that I almost felt a little guilty for how much fun that all was. She wanted to be sure I was there and asked for things to make her comfortable and told several people to look after me when she no longer could.

The next week things were fairly chaotic with both boys, their wives, the grandkids, Susan's sister Carol staying with me, our friend Renee coming, etc. etc. The memorial service was relaxed and meaningful and sweet, with the boys and me and my band and several old friends providing music that told of her extraordinary life and the "simple gifts" she gave us all (I'll attach the eulogy I wrote, in an Appendix). It all felt very unreal although I did feel some immediate relief I wasn't having to do things for her or think about her constantly. I kept waiting for the lapse to be over and her to show up again; but, she didn't. The normal thing to experience after a major loss, or any significant life milestone, is to feel off balanced and up in the air and a bit anxious. I have felt all of these and like I should be doing something responsible and productive, although this didn't extend to cleaning up and sorting out and catching up on chores long put off. I've processed everything through her mind and life and our relationship as well as my own mind for the past 45 years, so I have to learn to think a little differently and what to do with all the little things I used to tell her about or ask her opinion on. This morning I saw the first goldfinches of this Spring and an Indigo bunting at the feeder and immediately thought about telling her. On the other hand, I still think of big events or experiences regularly I want to call my parents and tell them about.....and they've been dead for years. Maybe that's part of the new relationship I have to forge with Susan. Everyone is now busy feeding me and recreating me, which I appreciate even if my waistline doesn't. But, I realize I now have to re-create part of myself that left along with Susan.

So, I guess this really is the end of the book. Thank you for going on this journey with me. I hope you found it informative, useful, supportive, educational and reassuring. Keep on keeping on; don't forget to tell your caregivee about the goldfinches; and **be good to yourself, my friend. You deserve it.**

APPENDIX: SUSAN EULOGY (my sister, Flo, read this for me at the memorial service)

I met Susan in the Fall of 1968 when my brother Bob and I moved into an apartment across from hers on the edge of the Baylor campus in Waco, Texas. We were friends of her roommate, Amber, who still comes to visit us yearly from Missouri. I liked all the roommates, but I was instantly drawn to Susan who, unfortunately, was dating some guy named Brian. She's never considered herself pretty, but I knew she was beautiful and in a very sweet way. Somehow her kind, loving spirit even showed up in her physical beauty to me. She had left the Baylor nursing school after fainting with her first couple of patients, and returned to Waco, abandoning her dreams to be a nurse in Viet Nam where she figured she'd probably die. Maybe something of an idealist? We had a class in the same building at the same time and I walked with her across campus every Monday, Wednesday and Friday. We became good friends and I asked her out as soon as Brian became history. As I sang in my Valentine's song to her years later, I was very taken with her simple caring, giving ways exemplified in her writing me and others little notes she painted on pieces of bark or little rocks or rusty tin can lids. She loved making Valentines and other cards for people until she no longer could years into her disabilities. That was a terrible loss for her and the rest of us.

She had to finish some classes after I graduated in 1969 and moved to Nashville for graduate school in clinical psychology. Susan was highly intelligent but not a great scholar as she was too busy working, taking care of her mother and sister long distance (her father had died unexpectedly the week of her high school graduation and one sister had a mental illness) and making cards and presents for everybody. Her Spanish teacher GAVE her a "D" as a present so she could graduate and the lab instructor was her close friend who got me started on guitar. A year later she moved to Nashville, too, to get her masters degree in social work at UT Nashville. Of course, she had to support herself in a variety of jobs. Our favorite was when she opened Exxon gas stations wearing a tiger suit ("Put a tiger in your tank") and giving out frozen chickens for a fill up. A year after that, we got married. I transferred to Baylor's graduate program and we moved back to Waco. She worked placing older children in adoption, a job she loved, and just a few months ago she had Nancy from my band track down a few of her favorite kids online as she still remembered them 35 years later. We moved to Birmingham in 1976 to do my one year internship at UAB and had Paul at the end of that year. I then went on to the UAB faculty. Soon thereafter my brother Bob moved here and eventually opened a private practice we shared for 25 years. David came along in 1980 and Susan eventually home schooled the boys from about 6th grade through high school. Her first friend here was Sabra and they went to a church called Believer's Chapel that met in a massage parlor. Several old parishioners from Believer's Chapel are here today and have remained devoted friends through all Susan's strokes, especially Genie and Jim and Sabra. After that church folded, Susan found her way to Grace and Truth, then Southside Mennonite, through Karen Mitchell when Larry Mitchell was pastor.

    Susan raised our boys in a 1977 Toyota station wagon we called "Old Blue," constantly driving them to youth groups, soccer, baseball, violin or piano lessons, home school play groups or classes, the art museum, art lessons, etc., etc. She taught them how to cook and sew and clean, how to make cards and presents for people and how to care for others. They visited sick people and took meals to new parents. She had them mow lawns for older people who couldn't and work in soup kitchens or on houses for Habitat for Humanity and they helped many people in church move. Susan also became very interested in gardening about that time and we all worked in her intensive raised bed French garden. She was so proud of it that even last year when we'd stopped working it 15 years ago, she wouldn't let me cut down the trees that had sprung up in it as they testified to how good the dirt was that she'd developed over years. Lets face it, Susan was just a nurturer, whether it was kids or friends or dirt and okra. Or husbands.

Susan did not have a good concept of who is a stranger and who is not. She viewed all strangers as friends she just didn't happen to know by name yet. The family myth was that she was incapable of going to the grocery store without coming back with someone's name, birthday, life story and current problems. I am shy but I learned to talk to strangers in stores and restaurants from her: one of the many, many things I learned from Susan. People called her regularly to seek advice and counsel as she was so compassionate, empathetic, understanding and accepting. That continued pretty much to the end of her life. She didn't let go of people very easily either. We still keep up with Paul's violin teachers from 20 years ago although they moved from here 10 years ago. We regularly talk to Sherry, whom she met the first day of first grade, and Amber, who introduced us in college, Janie, another college friend, and her roommate Renee who is with us this afternoon. She also attached to neighbors and has dearly loved Heather, Blake and Erin and their little girls, Rex and Lori and their families, Mary, Jimmy and Pitsa, Carolyn, Miss Virginia, Brian and his family, etc., etc. over the years, even when they moved away. They all loved her and have been wonderful neighbors for us and each other. Many of them are here today. The hardest thing for Susan in becoming so disabled was that she could no longer DO things for people: all the cards, mandarin orange chicken meals, flowers, notecards, homemade presents. It was hard for her to accept that she could always do what she did best anyway which was to care for others.

Susan loved beauty: flowers, art, music, pretty houses. But, she owned almost nothing. Her feeling was that she could go to the museum or symphony to see beauty whenever she wanted, and she took lots of kids with her to learn about beauty. But, she didn't want to actually own anything real nice until everyone in the world, her "friends or family whose names she didn't yet know," had at least the most essential things of food, shelter, clothing, etc. She convinced me to live as simple a life as possible in terms of house, entertainment, clothes, etc. She did have a fabulous collection of Willie Nelson CDs (Susan was not a Willie Nelson fan; she was THE Willie Nelson fan) and a number of videos she watched over and over, especially after she got where she couldn't see: *What About Bob? Man From Snowy River. Jane Eyre. Pride and Prejudice.* Her favorite was *A Man For All Seasons* because she so respected Thomas More's integrity and love of God and the truth that eventually cost him his head.

In 1995 I began to notice a number of disturbing changes in Susan. She began forgetting how to get to places and little things I'd told her or that had recently happened. She came back from a dental appointment in Riverchase by way of Sylacauga. She even forgot that the year before I'd gone to Texas for several days to buy a car from her beloved nephew, Jeff, who is here today with her other beloved nephew, Gil and their mother, her sister, Carol who was like a second mother to Susan, too. We went to a neurologist and started the million dollar workup, also getting a day of neuropsychological testing. The only reasonable conclusion was that she had Alzheimer's and we started planning for a life of gradual fading into oblivion. Almost five years later we found out through the kindness of one of my clients, about antiphospholipid antibody syndrome: an autoimmune disease that led to her having numerous little clotting strokes and accompanying loss of cognitive and bodily functioning. But, not Alzheimer's. We could prevent some with warfarin, the same chemical used in pest control, and she'd always ask me if I had given her her "rat poison" at pill time. As the years went on she lost more and more of her ability to see or do much of anything for herself. She tried to "bloom where you're planted" but she got more and more worn down. She worried about the burden she was to me and the family and about hurting my back or legs or arms and even in the hospital she was apologizing to the nurses for being so much trouble and asked if they were tired or she was hurting them. She had prayed for something to come along and take her to Heaven to see her mother and father and sister. Our granddaughter, Mari Carmen, comforted a grandson, Jack, by telling him that Grandma Susan was in Heaven making Valentines for people. She knew. This Wednesday Susan got her request and she died quietly and peacefully with David, Jennifer and me right at her side. I always saw Susan as a giver: in her little cards and little meals and little acts of service and little talks and her little bits of bark and stone and tin. True to form, Susan's favorite possession the past ten years has been her body donor card and she left her body to the UAB medical school where she can once again do and give for others. I've always seen the Shaker hymn, Simple Gifts, as somehow capturing the essence of Susan and the boys and I would like to do it for you now. Goodbye, Suze, and thank you.

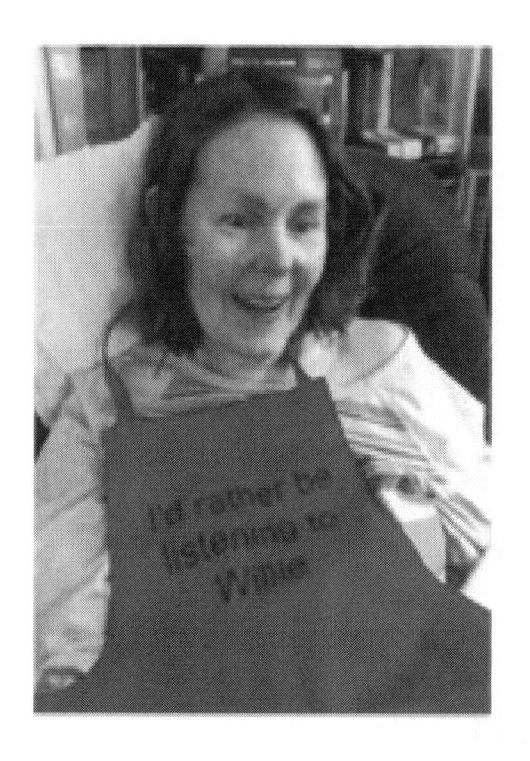

Susan Elizabeth Black Wendorf 12/03/1946 - 03/05/2014

Made in the USA
Columbia, SC
01 September 2020